Hope you find this
book helpful. Thanks
for your business!

BOOKS IN THE MERCIFULLY BRIEF, REAL WORLD SERIES

Raising Thousands (if Not Tens of Thousands) of Dollars with Email
by Madeline Stanionis • Emerson & Church, Publishers • $24.95

After reading the title of this book perhaps you're saying, "Sure, Red Cross and UNICEF can raise tons of money with email, but my agency isn't a brand name. You're telling me I can do the same!?" Author Madeline Stanionis isn't Pollyanna, but what she does convincingly show is that you can have surprising success if you approach email fundraising with a measure of intelligence and creativity.

Raising More Money with Newsletters than You Ever Thought Possible
by Tom Ahern • Emerson & Church, Publishers • $24.95

Today, countless organizations are raising more money with their newsletter than with traditional mail appeals. And after reading this book, it's easy to understand why. For starters, the newsletters Ahern shows you how to write deliver real news, not tired features. They make the donor feel important. They use emotional triggers to spur action. They're designed in a way to attract both browsers and readers. And they don't depend on dry statistics to make the organization's case.

Raising $1,000 Gifts by Mail
by Mal Warwick • Emerson & Church, Publishers • $24.95

Whoever heard of raising $1,000 gifts (not to mention $3,000, $4,000 and $5,000 gifts) by mail? That's the province of personal solicitation, right? Not exclusively, says Mal Warwick. With carefully selected examples and illustrations, Warwick shows you how to succeed with high-dollar mail, walking you step by step through the process of identifying your prospects, crafting the right letter, the right brochure, the right response device, and the right envelope.

Raising Money through Bequests
by David Valinsky & Melanie Boyd • Emerson & Church, Publishers • $24.95

Never in history has there been more money on the table for your organization than right now. Members of the "Greatest Generation" are in their later years, and as they pass on they're collectively leaving billions of dollars to charitable organizations. Their preferred vehicle for giving this money is the simple bequest – "I give and bequeath to...." With step by step guidance, and ample illustrations, this book shows you how to position your organization to be the beneficiary.

Attracting the Attention Your Cause Deserves
by Joseph Barbato • Emerson & Church, Publishers • $24.95

Think of Attracing the Attention Your Cause Deserves as a "Trade Secrets Revealed" book, one allowing you to accomplish three key objectives for your cause: greater visibility, a broader constituency, and more money raised. With more than a million nonprofit organizations in existence, there's a lot of noise out there. Shouting won't get you noticed - everyone's doing that. And everybody's tuning it out. What will attract attention is following Barbato's field-tested advice.

www.emersonandchurch.com

How to Raise
Planned Gifts by Mail

Emerson & Church
Real World Guides

First printed April 2008

10 9 8 7 6 5 4 3 2 1

Printed in the United States of America

This text is printed on acid-free paper.

Copies of this book are available from the publisher at discount when purchased in quantity.

Emerson & Church, Publishers
P.O. Box 338, Medfield, MA 02052
Tel. 508-359-0019
Fax 508-359-2703
www.emersonandchurch.com

Library of Congress Cataloging-in-Publication Data

Stelter, Larry.
  How to raise planned gifts by mail / Larry Stelter.
    p. cm.
  ISBN 1-889102-33-4 (pbk. : alk. paper)
  1. Direct-mail fund raising. 2. Deferred giving. I. Title.
  HV41.2.S74 2008
  658.15'224—dc22

                          2008001706

How to Raise Planned Gifts by Mail

LARRY STELTER

Emerson
& Church
PUBLISHERS

Of Related Interest
From Emerson & Church, Publishers

Never in history has there been more money on the table for your organization than right now.

Members of the "Greatest Generation" are in their 80s and 90s, and as they pass away they're collectively leaving billions of dollars to charitable organizations throughout the United States.

And their preferred vehicle for giving is the simple bequest – "I give and bequeath to…."

If at this very moment you're not marketing your bequest program with G force, you're missing what many are calling the greatest opportunity in the history of fundraising. To borrow a lyric from a "Greatest Generation" song, "Now is the hour."

Raising Money through Bequests lays out step by step how to establish a bequest program, how to work within your organization to strengthen and sustain it, how to market the program to the right audiences, and exactly what to do when responses start to come in.

Further, authors David Valinsky and Melanie Boyd supply plenty of sample materials you can immediately adapt. There's a brochure to introduce your program, a case for support that explains to prospective donors the merits of leaving a bequest, and a tasteful letter and folder that welcomes donors to the Bequest Society and describes its various features and benefits.

Additionally, you'll find sample bequest language to offer your donors, a sample agenda for a special gathering to introduce your bequest program, and even a list of possible names for your bequest society.

Raising Money through Bequests is a timely, uncomplicated book that can have a measurable impact on your organization's financial security.

Raising Money Through Bequests
How Your Organization Can Profit from the Biggest
Intergenerational Transfer of Wealth in History, 101 pp., $24.95,
by David Valinsky and Melanie Boyd

www.emersonandchurch.com

To my dad, Paul J. Stelter, for his faith in my judgment and vision to enter into the planned giving marketing arena in 1979. His encouragement has allowed us to build the largest planned giving marketing firm in the country which in turn has succeeded in helping thousands of nonprofit organizations fulfill their fundraising goals and further their important missions.

ABOUT THE AUTHOR

Larry Stelter is president and CEO of The Stelter Company, a national planned giving communications firm that focuses on print and Web products. The Stelter home office is in Des Moines, Iowa, with regional offices in Fort Worth, Texas, Chicago, Ill., Columbus, Ohio, Washington, D.C., Hartford, Conn. and Denver, Colo.

Founded in 1962, The Stelter Company and its staff of more than 80 individuals serve more than 2,500 print clients and 1,100 Web clients nationally.

Larry's primary responsibilities include project development and sales. He personally works with 300 clients in a 10-state territory. At many national and regional meetings, he has spoken on the subjects of planned giving marketing, Internet marketing, and relationship skills.

Larry is a graduate of the University of Iowa. He is married and the proud father of three sons (two 3rd-generation Stelters now working out of the Washington, D.C., and Denver offices). He serves on several boards, is an avid golfer and fisherman, and now is the proud grandpa of his first two grandsons – Ben and Sam.

CONTENTS

ABOUT THE AUTHOR

1   Getting to the heart of the matter   13

2   Keep your eyes on the goal   17

3   Who should receive my mailings?   25

4   Who *else* should receive my mailings?   29

5   Women in philanthropy   35

6   Targeting professional advisors   39

7   The direct mail package   45

8   The look   57

9   The message   63

10   Technically speaking   69

11   A matter of time   75

12   How to improve your gift planning program in five easy steps   79

13   What do you expect? The right way to measure success   83

14   Stay the course   87

APPENDIX

ACKNOWLEDGMENTS

1

Getting to the Heart of the Matter

——❖——

Even though you and I may never have met, I already know a good deal about you. Every single workday for the past 40 years, I've sat across the desk from, chatted on the phone with, or sent a note to gift planning professionals who want advice on creating a successful direct mail program.

Thousands of folks – confident, confused, fresh-faced, burnt-out – I've interacted with them all. And despite the differences between you and other gift planners, you inevitably share two desires:

1) You want to know the secret to closing more gifts sooner.

2) You want specific advice on what you should do today and tomorrow to make this happen.

As for Desire #1, here's "the secret" you've all been searching for: direct mail. *But* not just any direct mail, I hasten to add. You've got to send the right piece, whether it's a personal letter, a newsletter, or even a postcard.

Which is why, in support of Desire #2, I decided to write this book offering you step-by-step advice on creating and implementing a direct mail program that has been tested and really works.

CASE IN POINT

Mercy Hospital Foundation, Iowa City, Iowa

I'd love to lead off with a story about someone who launched a direct mail program that led to immediate planned gifts. If I did that, however, I'd be lying. So I'll begin instead with Julie Johnston, who I met a few years back, shortly after she was named president of the hospital foundation.

Julie's background had prepared her for the foundation presidency, but she admittedly knew nothing about developing a successful gift planning program. For several years, her predecessor sporadically mailed a cookie-cutter newsletter to a questionable mailing list. Of course, these efforts were met with limited response.

Luckily, Julie was quick to grasp what I call the *Track Star Plan*. A marathoner doesn't run a race and expect to win without preparing herself. She first commits to a plan of action that may include hiring a coach to train her, manage her progress, and encourage her to "stay the course." She may train for months or even years before she's prepared to achieve her goal.

As much as Julie wanted to sprint out of the blocks, she knew she needed to lay some groundwork using a proven plan for success, a process that took the better part of two years. The result? Within six months of reinvigorating her planned giving program, overall giving increased by 12 percent.

So, are you ready to get started? If so, over the next few chapters you'll discover how to:

• Win your boss's and board's support for your direct-marketing program.

- Create a mailing list that targets the people most likely to give.
- Set realistic expectations for your efforts.
- Develop a realistic budget.
- Avoid the most common roadblocks to success.
- Measure results the *right* way.

See you at the finish line!

2

Keep Your Eyes on the Goal

—❖—

An essential early step in developing your mailing is to agree upon its purpose. Understanding your goals gives order and structure to its content and helps you choose where to invest your time and energy.

Traditionally, to raise awareness and generate interest in planned giving, newsletters have been the vehicle of choice. But as the field of direct mail has grown, newsletters have had to compete with dozens of other pieces filling our donors' mailboxes. This has forced all of us to become far savvier in targeting our messages effectively and economically.

But let's not get ahead of ourselves. Before you can decide which approach is best for you, let's discuss the goals of your mailing. In my opinion, six in particular stand out:

Goal #1: Give Thanks

In his book *Mega Gifts*, Jerry Panas, a grandmaster of philanthropy who probably knows more about donors than anyone in America, stresses the principle of thanking individuals at least seven times for each gift they make. Seven times! I suspect most of us think that once or twice is enough. But Panas makes a valid case and his advice is certainly worth heeding, as a thanked donor is often a loyal (and increasingly) generous donor.

In terms of your mailings, this means placing your donors and their personal giving stories center stage. Is it any surprise that *People* magazine, with a circulation of nearly four million, ranks as one of the most successful magazine launches of the past 30 years?

People have a natural interest in reading stories about other people – especially heartwarming stories of triumph and generosity. What's more, donor stories not only help spur others toward similar acts of generosity, but the recognition quite often encourages repeat gifts.

CASE IN POINT

St. Olaf College, Northfield, Minn.

Grace Schroeder-Scott, director of special gifts, featured a story in the college's planned giving newsletter of a man who made a six-figure gift to the school. The donor was evidently so honored by the recognition that within 30 days of seeing his story in print, he made a second six-figure gift.

Goal #2: Educate

Planned gifts are sometimes called "stop-and-think gifts." They require more understanding and thought than it takes simply to write a check. Unfortunately, most people have little understanding of and devote even less thought to this type of giving. So before they can even consider making a planned gift, they need to be educated about estate planning. That's Job 1 for you, as we'll discuss in later pages.

CASE IN POINT

University of Iowa, Iowa City, Iowa

One of the most impressive educational tools we've ever developed is the one David Dierks, former director of planned giving, offered to members of his President's Circle as a thank-you for their past and current support. This group included a well-cultivated list of consistent, loyal donors whose giving history surpassed the $10,000 mark.

Formatted as a five-week, home study course, the program enticed enrollees by promising to teach them how to create a better will, cope with estate tax uncertainty, and boost income and cut taxes, among other important lessons. Upon completing the course, participants received a personal estate planning record book.

If only my teenage sons had been as excited about studying as the *31 percent* of people who responded to David's offer!

In the months right after the course, David and his staff dedicated much of their time to following up with everyone who enrolled. They were able to thank their supporters, make meaningful contacts, and continue to nurture those important relationships.

Goal #3: Generate Response

The key to securing planned gifts is building relationships, and direct mail serves as a springboard to cultivating potential donors. What can you offer donors that reflects your mission and will prompt them to respond now? An invitation to a free seminar on estate planning? Extended-access hours at your clinic? A white paper on how to cut taxes? A private tour of the museum's gardens?

The underlying motive here is to create an opportunity for a one-on-one conversation with your best prospects and to build the kind of trust and understanding that could eventually lead to a planned gift.

First-time responders, in particular, may need an extra-gentle touch. Whatever you do, don't try to land a gift immediately! Prospective donors must trust you and have a thorough understanding of your work – a process that could take months or even years – before they'll consider a meaningful gift. With first-time responders, ask about their connection with your organization and uncover why they made the effort to request the information. Be sure to set a follow-up date and think of another reason to make contact.

CASE IN POINT

All it Takes Is One Response

The number of leads you generate with your mailings is never as important as how you handle the opportunity to contact the donor. A development director at a Rhode Island hospital received only two responses from an issue of a newsletter. His results, however, were spectacular – he closed a $500,000 charitable gift annuity, and three years later the same donor created a $9.5 million charitable remainder unitrust.

In contrast, a development director at a California hospital received 250 reply cards from his quarterly mailing, but felt dissatisfied with the responses. When I asked whether those who responded were good prospects, he said he hadn't had time to call any of them; he simply mailed the booklets they requested. He didn't fulfill his obligation by completing the most important part of the development process – following up with his organization's most interested patrons.

Goal #4: Motivate Donors to Seek Professional Advice

Another way to open the doors to more planned gifts is to motivate your potential donors to seek the advice of their professional advisors. Many people who receive your mailings won't respond directly to you; rather, they'll first call their attorney or financial advisor to discuss estate planning and gift options. That's why it's key to build relationships with professional advisors in your community and educate them about the value of gift planning, as they may be fielding questions on your behalf. If you get a call from an attorney asking for your legal bequest language or for more information on giving opportunities, take notice.

CASE IN POINT

Mankato State University, Mankato, Minn.

One day, Bob Goldberg, director of planned giving at Mankato State University (now Minnesota State University, Mankato), received a letter from an attorney in Rochester, Minn., asking him to confirm the legal bequest language for the university foundation. The letter was sent to a P.O. Box Bob had created specifically to track responses.

Intrigued, Bob called the attorney and learned that an MSU alumna and her husband had visited the attorney with Bob's newsletters in hand. Within the margins, the couple had scribbled notes and questions.

Even though the attorney had referred to such newsletters as "junk mail," Bob was happy with the bottom-line results: The alumna left $500,000 to MSU and her husband did the same for his alma mater, the University of St. Thomas.

Goal #5: Break the Ice

Direct mail programs also serve to break the ice with your donors. Those who are receiving your regular communications are normally more open to your request for a planned gift. Take a lesson from business studies on lead generation, which have found that companies with a high level of awareness have a far easier time generating leads than companies that continually have to introduce themselves to prospects.

By integrating your tactics – making "soft" phone calls, sending direct mail, sponsoring events, and keeping touch via emails – you'll be warming the prospective donor to respond positively to your "ask."

CASE IN POINT

Pomona College, Claremont, Calif.

Several years ago, I worked with Howard Metzler, then director of trusts and estates at Pomona College. At the time, Howard had a staff of five planned giving officers assigned to visit one on one with an extremely qualified list of donors and prospects. The group also received a quarterly newsletter from the department.

Howard's team noted that the donors they met with were unusually receptive to their personal visits. On more than one occasion, donors greeted the planned giving officers with a stack of past newsletters in one hand and a list of questions in the other.

Goal #6: Drive Readers to Your Website

As seniors discover the Internet in ever-increasing numbers, the Web has emerged as an important and cost-effective way to educate donors about gift planning. Cross-promote your website in your mailings and you'll create a powerful partnership between Web and print.

Many donors find the anonymity and self-service aspects of the Web quite appealing. They can read gift planning articles at their leisure, access online gift calculators, make online donations, and learn more about the needs and successes of your organization.

And while you'll probably never know for sure how many people read past the first line of your print communication, you can track activity on your website at a granular level – getting information on which articles are most popular, and learn how much time people spend with particular pieces of content.

CASE IN POINT

St. Mary's Duluth Clinic, Duluth, Minn.

My company publishes the quarterly planned giving newsletter for St. Mary's Duluth Clinic Foundation. We also created and host the foundation's Internet home page and gift planning content. I'm constantly coaching my clients to leave room in their mailings for a significant ad promoting their website, so I was pleased to see that Executive Director Steven Johnston included one in his most recent issue. When a month later I reviewed Steve's report, I discovered that in the four days following his newsletter mailing, more than 155 new visitors accessed his website.

I called Steve to share the great news. He was particularly excited because he'd previously judged the success of his mailing on the handful of reply cards he typically received. Had Steve not factored in his website activity, he would never have known that the combined response rate of his print and website effort was more than 11 percent.

•••

As the title of this chapter is "Keeping Your Eyes on the Goal," let me end with one of my favorite examples of allegiance to a goal. One day Albert Einstein and his assistant needed a paper clip. They found one but it was too mangled to use, so they began searching for a tool to straighten it.

Just then Einstein came across a box of paper clips in his desk drawer and proceeded to shape a new clip into the desired tool to fix the mangled one. When his confused assistant asked him why he was bothering with this step, Einstein replied: "Once I am set on a goal, it becomes difficult to deflect me."

Take a cue from the famed mathematician and keep your eyes on the prize.

3

Who Should Receive My Mailings?

Unlike holiday greetings and change of address notifications, your planned giving mailings shouldn't be showered on the general population. Direct marketers often cite the 60-30-10 formula for determining a mailing's success.

Sixty percent depends on the quality of the mail list; 30 percent is based on the content of the appeal; and 10 percent can be attributed to the design or format. Since marketing dollars are precious and your board's expectations for results are high, don't dilute your efforts by mailing to anyone other than your best prospects.

Let's make it simple. Start by limiting your list to people who have met one basic criterion: Anyone who has made at least *two* gifts of any size to your organization (more about this in a minute).

Note some of the folks who will *not* make the cut:

• Wealthy, philanthropic people in your community who have never given to your organization.

• Everyone who attended your last auction, had a few drinks and spent more than they intended.

• People who have made only a *single* contribution of any amount.

• Your parents, friends or random family members who, again, fail to meet the basic criterion (OK, you can include your mom).

Once you've assembled an initial list, refine it based on the following characteristics.

• Age

Age 55 is a magic number in the gift planning business. It's the point, we've determined, where people seem most open to learning about and acting on philanthropic opportunities. The sight of their AARP card no longer stings, retirement is a welcome topic, their kids are leaving or already gone, they're ready to burn the mortgage papers, and a fair amount of sentimentality is setting in.

If you're largely clueless about the age of the people in your database, consider conducting an age overlay. This involves matching your list of names and addresses against those on a list provided by a company specializing in gathering key data on households nationwide. These companies pull information from various public sources and can help you fill in the gaps without violating any privacy laws.

• Loyalty and Affinity

Perhaps you're wondering why it's important to mail only to people who have made a second gift. People make donations for lots of reasons: peer pressure at a golf event, as a memorial for an elderly neighbor, or because an adorable five-year-old knocked on the door asking. Typically, before donors are willing to make a planned gift, they must be connected – in most cases passionately connected – to the work and future of your organization and believe they can have a real impact on your mission. The best indicator of this is continuing support, not a one-shot gift.

It's tempting, I know, to include the entire class of '73 or that sweet couple who have attended the annual gala for the past two years. But if they haven't made a single donation, don't waste your limited marketing dollars soliciting them for planned gifts.

• Size of Gifts

Note that when I suggested you mail to people who have made at least two gifts I said gifts of any amount. Yes, *any* amount. I've yet to find any statistical data correlating the size of a donor's annual gift to his or her potential to make a planned gift. This is true, in part, because most planned gifts are made from assets (e.g. appreciated securities, retirement plan assets or real estate holdings) rather than yearly income.

Further, planned gift donors come from all walks of life, not just wealthy backgrounds. We've all heard stories about the small donor who gave $25 per year for 20 years, then quietly left his or her entire multimillion-dollar estate to charity.

I've seen both extremes when analyzing an organization's planned giving mailing list. Some are too broad in scope – including too many people without a strong connection to the organization. Others are too narrow – including only those donors who are very old or have previously given a very large gift.

CASE IN POINT
The Cost of Setting the Bar Too High

I worked with a hospital that had been mailing a planned giving newsletter for several years with little response. I asked the development director who was on the mailing list. The hospital was definitely working the 55 and older crowd, but its loyalty criterion was a bit off. It had a minimum level of $2,500 in annual giving before donors were put on the mailing list!

I explained that the profile of a planned giving donor includes more than the wealthy and suggested the hospital expand its list. About 18 months later, I bumped into the development director, who reported that responses more than doubled since dropping the $2,500 minimum.

■ Help! I Can't Afford My Mailing List

When money is a major constraint, narrow your list according to the following formula:

• Pull the records for prospects aged 55 or older and look for donors who, in terms of their giving history, strike a balance between longevity and consistency. For example, pull the names of anyone who appears on your annual giving rolls for three of the last five years. Can you afford to mail to that list?

• If the answer is no, then narrow the list further to those people aged 55 or older who have made at least four gifts at any time in the past seven years.

• If you're still over budget, focus on those who have made gifts in *five* of the past *eight* years or mail to those who are age 60 or older instead of 55.

In short, keep experimenting until you reach a target list size that falls within your budget.

4

Who *Else* Should Receive My Mailings?

———❖———

Although a donor's age and giving history should be the primary components when winnowing your mailing list, don't forget about groups with special affiliation that often fly below the radar. In previous pages I've preached the two-gift rule. That is, don't bother soliciting people for planned gifts who have made only a single gift – your resources will best be directed elsewhere.

However, within several of the following groups I'm willing to eat my words. There are certain non-givers whose unique commitment to your mission makes them viable candidates for a planned gift.

The two-gift rule is thereby dispensed with for ... volunteers, board members, and staff people. For two other special groups, small business owners and people regularly attending your special events, the situation isn't as clear.

• Volunteers

Volunteers give their time, which many see as a substitute for making a financial gift. Their reasoning is this: "I can't afford a gift of cash, but I'll donate one Saturday a month to help with building maintenance." By this logic, a volunteer who makes consistent donations of time is probably a good candidate for a future planned gift.

Recently my company conducted focus groups nationwide with people who have made bequests. From our research, we've confirmed that planned gifts are almost always inspired by a personal connection to the organization. Since volunteering accelerates that connection by providing hands-on experience, I feel volunteers are a group deserving special consideration.

• Board Members

If you expect board members to make a planned gift to your organization – and I certainly hope you do – then I suggest you strive for 100 percent participation from those who have served more than four years. In addition to generating revenue for your organization, that you can demonstrate board support will burnish your credibility when approaching others for a planned gift.

• Legacy Society Members

Many organizations have recognition clubs, often referred to as Legacy or Heritage Societies, for people who have made a planned gift. Membership in these groups provides unique privileges and is an excellent way of strengthening your relationship with key donors.

You want to keep mailing to this group for at least two reasons: 1) To continue to assure the person that your organization is a solid investment – nothing sours a relationship like neglect; 2) With continued education and nurturing, a generous donor may decide to become an extraordinarily generous donor in the future.

Keep in mind that some may decline membership in your heritage society even though they qualify. Be sure to mail to everyone who has made a planned gift, not just society members.

CASE IN POINT

The Wrath of the Ignored Donor

After a friend of mine included a charity in her will, the organization went on radio silence – no more newsletters, no more invitations to events, no more love. Other organizations she recognized in her will maintained faithful contact, however. After several years of continued neglect from Charity No. 1, my friend backtracked to her attorney and stripped the organization from her will.

• Retired or Tenured Staff

If you represent a college, university or hospital, you probably have the strongest loyalty from retired professors, doctors, nurses, and other staff. Early in their careers, these individuals are often too busy outfitting their kids with braces, saving for a down payment on a new home, or installing a family pool to become regular, generous donors. Now that they've passed the magical age of 55, however, it's time to rekindle their allegiance to your cause.

It's acceptable to depart from the two-gift, consistency-of-giving rules when adding long-term employees to your mailing list. Like volunteers, employees may equate their loyal service to your organization as a gift in itself.

CASE IN POINT

Heroes Among Us

Years ago my son, Nathan, heard an inspiring story about a janitor who for more than 30 years worked at an independent school outside of Washington, D.C.

Apparently, the janitor had no spouse or children – his family was the school and the students and faculty he cared so much about. Upon his death, school officials learned that this loyal employee had left the school a bequest of nearly $125,000!

Herein lies a noteworthy example of why it's important not to overlook people who have spent their lives dedicated to your organization in any capacity, whether they're staff, faculty, or volunteers.

• Business Owners

Your database may include privately held businesses that have given more than once to your annual fund or capital campaign. A business, however, isn't a prospect for a planned gift – it can't die and leave you its vacation home in Phoenix. Instead, you'll need to work to develop a relationship with the person who approved the original gift – oftentimes the owner.

Because gift planning requires personal reflection and deliberation, always mail to a donor's home address. You don't want to compete with a donor's Franklin Covey planner for attention.

• Special Event Participants

Let's revisit those people who have sustained their loyalty over the years but haven't made a gift outside of a special event. These are the folks who buy tickets to the holiday gala, play in every golf tournament, and show up in the rain for the annual walk. Are they worthwhile prospects for planned gifts?

The answer is maybe. I'm not suggesting you automatically add these people to your mailing list, but I am suggesting you make an effort to determine their commitment to your organization.

Try to thank these people face-to-face for their participation and attendance. In that way, you'll be able to assess whether their presence is more from a civic duty or from a genuine passion for your mission. If the latter is evident, include them in your planned giving list.

5

Women in Philanthropy

———❖———

I graduated from college in 1970, three years before tennis great Billie Jean King topped Bobby Riggs in the infamous "Battle of the Sexes." The equal rights movement was undoubtedly the prevailing women's story of my day. Nearly 40 years later, that movement has paved the way for an initiative of a different kind: the women's philanthropy movement.

With women now controlling more than half of the personal wealth in the United States and growing increasingly comfortable in their role as financial decision-makers, organizations need to fully recognize the great potential in cultivating and inspiring their women donors.

According to The Center on Philanthropy at Indiana University:

• Single women are significantly more likely than single men to make a philanthropic gift.

• Married men are more likely to give and to make larger gifts than single men, suggesting that women's charitable tendencies influence their husbands.

• Women who participate in donor education programs are more likely to give larger gifts, to give unrestricted gifts, to develop long-term giving plans, and to hold leadership positions on nonprofit boards.

In addition, single women likely make up a growing portion of your 65-and-older audience. According to U.S. Census Bureau data, more than 75 percent of women aged 85 and older are widowed, compared with 42 percent of men in the same age group.

A combination of factors drives this statistic, including longer life expectancies for women, the tendency for women to marry slightly older men, and higher remarriage rates for older widowed men than widowed women.

Here's something else relevant to your pursuit of women's philanthrophy. In focus groups my company recently conducted, we heard loud and clear from donors and potential donors of all ages that gift planning mailings, to be effective, must closely mirror how individuals view themselves: in age and physical appearance, financial status, interest, and values.

If, for example, the people featured seemed too old or too rich in comparison to the reader, he or she was strongly turned off by the materials. Our findings support other tests that show the benefits of understanding your audience and fine-tuning your mailings to their personal preferences.

A few years ago, the New York City-based American Society for the Prevention of Cruelty to Animals (ASPCA) segmented its donors into three groups: dog lovers, cat lovers, and unknown. People who received emails featuring targeted material (cute cat photos and cat-related text for cat lovers; dog photos and dog-related text for dog lovers) gave nearly double the amount as people who received the generic mix of dog and cat stories.

How do you apply the principles of segmentation to your mailings to your female donors? First, I suggest pulling together a group of women supporters who are representative of the audience you're trying to cultivate. Ask them about what they'd most like to see in your planned giving mailings. Arm yourself with plenty of examples, including newsletters, postcards, brochures, and other types of direct mail solicitations. What types of pictures appeal to them most? Which design styles do they find most attractive? What turns them off?

Set aside your own preconceived ideas about what your audience requires. Listen carefully to their preferences and to the specific language they use to express themselves.

For example, a woman in one of our focus groups said, "I'm not rich. I want to feel like my gift, no matter how small, can make a difference." I immediately instructed one of our writers to include this very language in a gift-planning newsletter. The article began: "You don't have to be rich to make a difference in the lives of others. Even a small gift …."

CASE IN POINT

Giving Voice to Women Donors

During her tenure as director of planned giving at Kansas State University in Manhattan, Kansas, Sandi Fruit divided her mailing list into two groups. One list consisted of single women donors age 45 and older, and the second "a much larger list" included all other donors, male and female, age 50 and older.

The women-only list received a specialized women's gift planning newsletter; the other list received a traditional gender-neutral newsletter. After three issues, the women's newsletter pulled seven to eight times more leads than the traditional newsletter.

As Sandi developed relationships with these women, she learned that previously many of them felt ignored by the university; it wasn't until they received several issues of the gender-slanted newsletter that they gained enough trust and confidence to respond.

Despite the proven value of marketing specifically to women, I suspect few organizations take this approach. A survey of our client base a few years back revealed that fewer than 15 percent compiled separate mailing lists targeting women donors.

If your time and budget allow, creating a planned giving mailing targeted to women will likely deliver impressive results. For despite Bobby Riggs' assertions to the contrary, at least when it comes to philanthropy, women may very well be the greater sex.

6

Targeting Professional Advisors

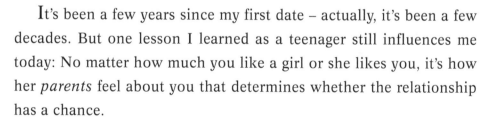

It's been a few years since my first date – actually, it's been a few decades. But one lesson I learned as a teenager still influences me today: No matter how much you like a girl or she likes you, it's how her *parents* feel about you that determines whether the relationship has a chance.

This same principle holds true in the gift planning world. If a donor's most trusted advisors are confused about, intimidated by, or ignorant of the concept of gift planning, they have the potential to quash the donor's most heartfelt overtures.

Just to be clear, when I mention advisors, I'm including the professionals who may influence the transfer of a client's assets to your organization:

• Attorneys who specialize in wills and trusts, probate or estate planning

• CPAs and tax accountants

- Financial planners and financial advisors
- Bankers and trust officers
- Stockbrokers
- Life insurance agents
- Real estate agents

Cultivating a relationship with professional advisors is akin to spending time watching sports with your girlfriend's dad or helping her mom clean up the dishes after dinner. Your actions should demonstrate respect and competence. The ultimate goal is to bring these professionals closer to your organization and educate them about gift planning techniques.

Advisors will be more likely to endorse your gift proposals if they understand the various charitable techniques available, if they've met you and feel you have donors' best interests at heart, and if they recognize your organization as a sound financial steward.

Alternatively, an advisor who is unfamiliar with charitable planning can act as a gatekeeper when a client asks for input on your gift proposal. Instead of saying, "I'm unfamiliar with that technique ... Let me get back to you," the advisor's pride might lead him or her to say: "That's not really a good idea for you."

One aside: Some development officers expect professional advisors to recommend their organizations to clients. That expectation is unrealistic and fraught with moral and ethical implications. Your goal should be to build a genuine, professional relationship based on shared knowledge. Then, when the right circumstances present themselves, the advisor is prepared to support a client's wishes and provide appropriate direction.

CASE IN POINT

Matching Donors to Mission

My staff estate planning attorney, Johni Hays, J.D., regularly hosts seminars for gift planners interested in cultivating relationships with professional advisors. Johni has worked with Child*Serve,* an organization providing rehabilitation services and skilled care to medically fragile children.

She remembers well the day a prominent local attorney approached her after a presentation at Child*Serve* headquarters. "I've got a client who's specifically interested in helping children with special needs," he said, "and I'm planning to tell her about what I learned today." Within days, the donor had initiated a planned gift with Child*Serve* that approached seven figures.

Cheri Burns, director of development at Child*Serve,* has had similar experiences. Recently, a professional advisor with whom Cheri regularly communicates mentioned he had used what he'd learned through her professional advisor education program to help a philanthropically inclined client make a $100,000 gift to the organization.

■ Finding Professional Advisors

To begin developing a list of professional advisors in your community, visit the National Association of Estate Planners & Councils at www.naepc.org for a listing of councils nearest you. Members will consist of CPAs, financial advisors, trust officers, and attorneys.

Next, go to www.martindalehubble.com for a list of probate and estate planning attorneys in your community. Contact the state bar association to request a listing of local attorneys who are members of the probate and tax divisions.

Some states have a trust officers' association from which you can obtain a list of the members' names. In addition, most financial planners belong to the Financial Planning Association. Visit www.fpanet.org to find the names of local members. Many life insurance professionals belong to the Society of Financial Service

Professionals. Go to www.financialpro.org to search for members.

■ Cultivating Professional Advisors

Thankfully, many of the methods commonly used to court professional advisors require little cash outlay and actually work in tandem with strategies used to cultivate donors. Consider these ideas:

1) Ask them to serve on your board or planned giving committee.

2) Ask them to serve on estate planning seminar panels.

3) Ask them to be resource attorneys for wills clinics.

4) Invite them to attend a seminar hosted by your organization to update professional advisors on charitable giving tax laws and techniques, and to earn continuing education credits. (It's best to hire an outside speaker to conduct the lecture.)

5) Periodically send them articles or newsletters to keep them abreast of estate planning and charitable planning issues. If your budget allows, create a publication specifically geared to professional advisors. An e-newsletter is a low-cost option for this segment.

6) Plan quarterly or semi-annual luncheons with selected professional advisors in the community. Have your president or a key board member serve as host.

■ Materials for Professionals

One of the most effective ways of building relationships with professional advisors – though admittedly not viable for smaller organizations – is to incorporate these individuals into your mailing program. But, understand, professional advisors shouldn't receive the same materials as your donor. Advisors need correspondence with a tone, style, and call to action that suits their specific needs.

Take a newsletter, for example. For your donor, such a piece would include a heartwarming testimonial on how donations have helped a particular person, beginner-level guidance on estate planning techniques, and broad-strokes articles on the most popular ways to making a planned gift.

In contrast, an advisor's newsletter might offer an advanced-level analysis of a single gift vehicle or charitable technique. The language and content would assume the reader has a professional understanding of basic estate planning and financial planning concepts – thus dispensing with elementary information and getting right to the meat. Footnotes referencing appropriate sections of the Internal Revenue Code and citations to applicable case law would be provided here as well.

■ What to Do When the Phone Rings

If a professional advisor contacts you and asks for your organization's legal name, that's normally a sign that he or she has a client who's drafting a will or trust agreement.

Of course you'd like to know the name of the client – and there's no harm in asking - but an advisor usually won't disclose this.

Once you've provided the advisor with the information, prepare a follow-up mailing. Resend your organization's legal bequest language along with information on your planned giving recognition club. The advisor may be willing to pass along the information to the donor. Such subtle influence from an intermediary might prompt the donor to inform you of his or her plans, allowing you to nurture this relationship further.

7

The Direct Mail Package

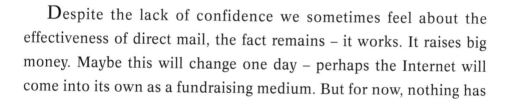

Despite the lack of confidence we sometimes feel about the effectiveness of direct mail, the fact remains – it works. It raises big money. Maybe this will change one day – perhaps the Internet will come into its own as a fundraising medium. But for now, nothing has replaced the tried-and-true formula I'm about to outline here.

The rub for gift planning professionals is that results might not come to fruition for quite a while. Frustrating? Heck, yes. But it's a medium you can't afford to ignore.

As you create your direct mail package, keep in mind the goals I outlined in Chapter 2:

   1) Give thanks
   2) Educate
   3) Generate response
   4) Motivate donors to seek professional advice
   5) Break the ice
   6) Drive readers to your website

■ Variety is the spice

In our field, the standard direct mail package consists of four items: the cover letter, the newsletter or brochure, the offer, and the reply device. But even that's in flux, as organizations today are experimenting with postcards, self-mailers, "telegrams," and other formats in an effort to reduce "fatigue" and capture attention.

Good thing, too, as research sponsored by my company suggests that gift planners who use a variety of ways to promote their program experience better results.

In our survey of more than 650 organizations that took advantage of the Pension Protection Act of 2006 to promote IRA gifts, nearly one-in-five used multiple methods of doing so. The extra effort paid off, showering these organizations with more responses, more closed gifts, and more funds overall. In addition, they were more likely to attract new donors.

Of the group surveyed, newsletter mailings were the most popular method of promotion, followed by personal letters and Web content. Twenty-eight percent promoted in ways not specifically asked about in this survey. These included ideas such as placing articles and ads in magazines, and mailing brochures and article clippings on the subject.

Method of Promotion	Total
Newsletters	56%
Personal letters	41%
Web content	34%
Postcards	16%
E-mail	16%
Other	28%

■ The Components

Let's now take a closer look at the components of the stardard mail package. Some version of this should form the core of your gift planning marketing program.

• *The Outer Envelope*

Like the clothes you wear, the mailing envelope you choose is your first opportunity to make an impression and is the most important piece of your mailer. According to the Direct Marketing Association's Statistical Fact Book, 70 percent of respondents to one survey said the name of the sender and return address is the No. 1 reason they open an envelope.

Illustration No. 1: Outer envelope for The Cleveland Orchestra

Unlike credit card solicitors and catalog retailers who troll for new business by purchasing lists of potential customers, your mailings are directed to regular donors who have already expressed an affinity for

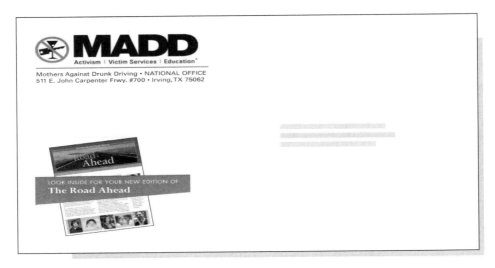

Illustration No. 2: Outer envelope for Mothers Against Drunk Driving

Illustration No. 3: Outer envelope for the Children's Hospital and Health System

your organization and its mission. Use the outer envelope to reinforce your brand and help these loyal donors quickly recognize the sender.

• *The Cover Letter*

Including an introductory letter with your mailing costs pennies and historically has proven to lift results significantly. Your letter, typically printed on your organization's letterhead, should read like a conversation

Dallas K. Beal
Legacy Society

Name   Fall 2007
Address
Address

Greetings!

Remember fall in Fredonia? It's hard to imagine a more beautiful setting. I hope you are enjoying a relaxing, fun-filled season, wherever you call home. In addition to the delightful weather and the changing color of the leaves, autumn in Fredonia means welcoming 5,500 students to the community and our campus. As new and returning students arrived, the excitement of a new academic year was contagious. I'm proud to say that my daughter is a 3-1-3 student at SUNY Fredonia this year, making the experience truly personal.

As I reminisced about my own college days (having a college-age daughter does that to you), I couldn't help but wonder how many young people don't have the opportunity to experience that kind of excitement because of financial concerns. That is why we are so thankful to you, our alumni and friends, who, through your generosity, make the load lighter for so many people seeking higher education.

In this issue of the *Dallas K. Beal Legacy Society* newsletter, a very special alumnus, Ralph Serpe, '85, reminds us that it is never too early to think about giving back for an education he found so valuable. At age 25 Ralph named SUNY Fredonia in his first will. Subsequently, he also named Fredonia as a beneficiary of his retirement plan. For Ralph, his estate plan is a very personal way to honor those important to him.

Bequests and retirement plan beneficiary designations are wonderful vehicles to create a legacy without affecting your current financial situation. In this issue, I have provided some general information for you to consider as you create or update your own estate plans. If you would like more information on how to strengthen your plans while benefiting your loved ones and SUNY Fredonia, feel free to call or write anytime. Thoughtful planning will not only reduce your tax burden, but it will also help ensure the success of SUNY Fredonia students in future generations.

For Fredonia alumni who graduated in 1984 and 1985 who may be receiving the *Dallas K. Beal Legacy Society* newsletter for the first time, I hope you find it helpful. Since so many of you remember Ralph from those special days, we thought you might be interested in this particular issue.

As always, your inquiries are confidential and there is no obligation. Feel free to give me a call at 716-673-3321, e-mail me at betty.gossett@fredonia.edu or return the enclosed reply card in the envelope provided with this newsletter. I'd love to hear from you!

Warm regards,

Betty C Gossett

Betty Catania Gossett, '76

Fredonia College Foundation • 272 Central Avenue • Fredonia, NY 14063 • 716-673-3321

Illustration No. 4: Cover letter from Fredonia College's Dallas K. Beal Legacy Society

between you and your most valued friends and donors. This is your opportunity to introduce yourself and to reiterate your organization's mission and needs, and to offer a compelling reason for the recipient to respond to your request.

Almost needless to say, letters should be personalized and include a

Thomas
COLLEGE

Dear Friend,

George Bernard Shaw, an Irish author, once said, "I am of the opinion that my life belongs to the community, and as long as I live it is my privilege to do for it whatever I can."

As an alumnus of Thomas College, you are part of a community that grows bigger each year. When you graduated from Thomas, your class may have consisted of 20-30 students. This fall's entering class was the largest in College history—we welcomed 253 first-year students.

Students are joining the Thomas College Community because they know that a degree from Thomas will open doors for them. 73% of these students are first generation college students. They understand the importance of a college degree. In the current economic climate, an education beyond the 12th grade level is essential for men and women to compete professionally. They come to Thomas to be taught the skills necessary to become professionals, and to become valuable contributors to their communities. At Thomas we provide skills that will last a lifetime. We back it up with our guaranteed job placement program—the only one of its kind in the nation.

As a member of the Thomas Community, one of the ways you can help is by sharing your Thomas experience with family, friends and colleagues. Each time you do, you are opening new doors and opportunities for them. In a sense, you are inviting them to join our community.

I am inviting you to join another community. This community is made up of individuals who are well-informed and educated about estate planning. A few months back I sent you your first publication on estate planning. I hope you found it useful. I am enclosing a second publication that covers another very important topic—the anatomy of a will.

I hope our estate planning publications prove to be helpful to you. Please call 207.859.1167, or e-mail dumontc@thomas.edu for more information.

Sincerely,

Cathy M. Dumont
Manager for Annual & Planned Giving

P.S. Please note that you only have until Dec. 31, 2007 to give under the Pension Protection Act of 2006.

www.thomas.edu   180 West River Road Waterville, ME 04901   207-859-1111

Illustration No. 5: Cover letter from Thomas College

live signature, as doing so can sometimes lift the response by 20 percent or more. Personal touches such as a handwritten note in the margin ("I hope you can make it to the seminar next month") reinforce the idea that the recipient is receiving your special attention. In addition, remember to include a P.S. – usually the best-read component of any letter.

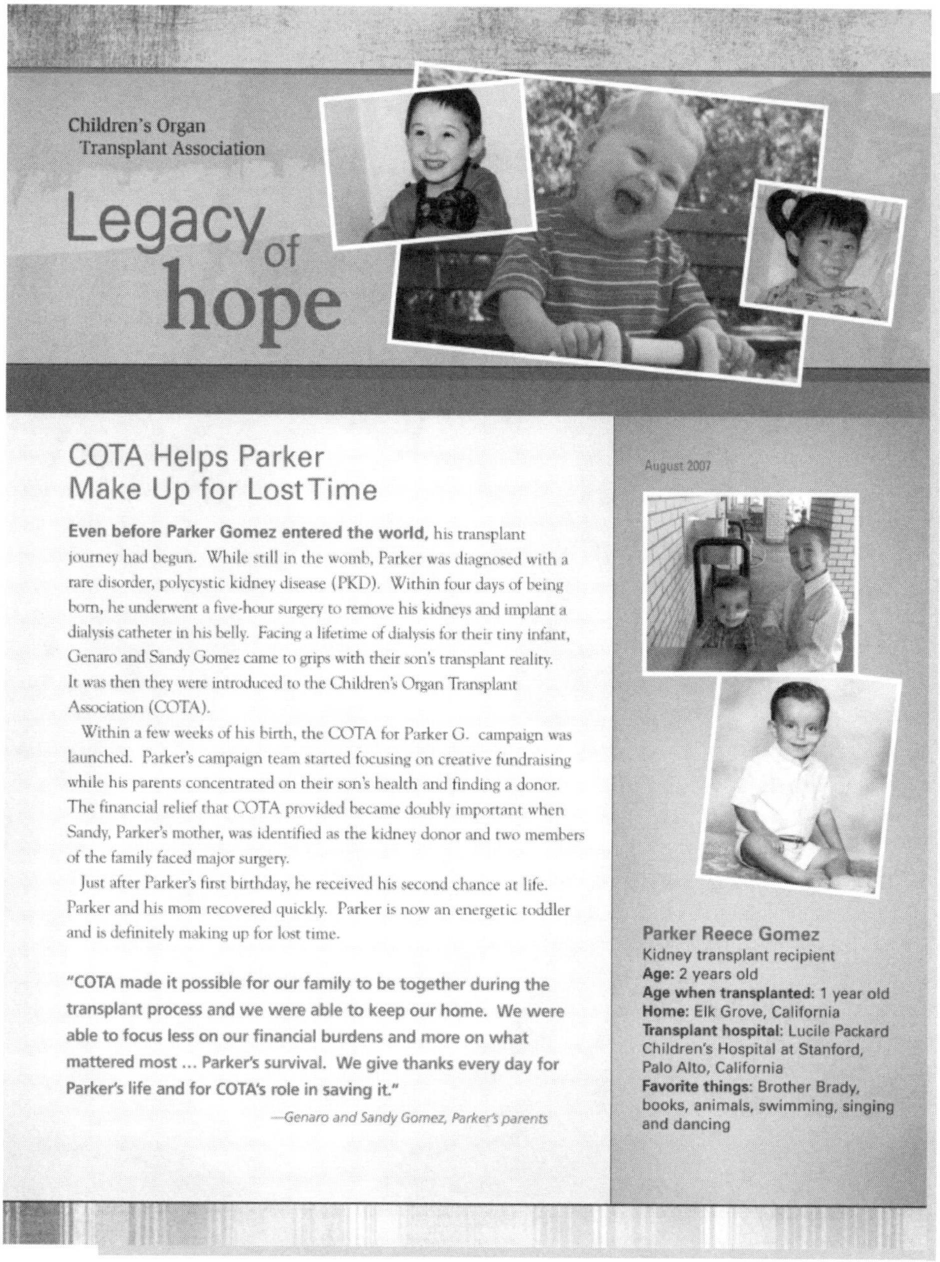

Children's Organ Transplant Association

Legacy of hope

COTA Helps Parker Make Up for Lost Time

August 2007

Even before Parker Gomez entered the world, his transplant journey had begun. While still in the womb, Parker was diagnosed with a rare disorder, polycystic kidney disease (PKD). Within four days of being born, he underwent a five-hour surgery to remove his kidneys and implant a dialysis catheter in his belly. Facing a lifetime of dialysis for their tiny infant, Genaro and Sandy Gomez came to grips with their son's transplant reality. It was then they were introduced to the Children's Organ Transplant Association (COTA).

Within a few weeks of his birth, the COTA for Parker G. campaign was launched. Parker's campaign team started focusing on creative fundraising while his parents concentrated on their son's health and finding a donor. The financial relief that COTA provided became doubly important when Sandy, Parker's mother, was identified as the kidney donor and two members of the family faced major surgery.

Just after Parker's first birthday, he received his second chance at life. Parker and his mom recovered quickly. Parker is now an energetic toddler and is definitely making up for lost time.

"COTA made it possible for our family to be together during the transplant process and we were able to keep our home. We were able to focus less on our financial burdens and more on what mattered most ... Parker's survival. We give thanks every day for Parker's life and for COTA's role in saving it."

—Genaro and Sandy Gomez, Parker's parents

Parker Reece Gomez
Kidney transplant recipient
Age: 2 years old
Age when transplanted: 1 year old
Home: Elk Grove, California
Transplant hospital: Lucile Packard Children's Hospital at Stanford, Palo Alto, California
Favorite things: Brother Brady, books, animals, swimming, singing and dancing

Illustration No. 6: Educational device from Children's Organ Transplant Association

• *The Educational Device*

As we saw from the survey on p. 46, a donor newsletter is a prime way to keep in touch with and stay connected to your planned giving

ST. JUDE

FRIENDS IN HOPE

SPRING 2007

St. Jude Children's Research Hospital
ALSAC • Danny Thomas, Founder

Finding cures. Saving children.

A FINANCIAL AND CHARITABLE PLANNING GUIDE FOR FRIENDS OF ST. JUDE

BRADY BURFORD'S PARENTS FIND HOPE AT ST. JUDE

Heather and Dru Burford's memories of their son's cancer diagnosis in December 2005 are intertwined with those of the Christmas holiday. After little Brady's first trip to see Santa, he developed symptoms indicative of a stomach virus. When the symptoms persisted, Heather and Dru took Brady to a pediatrician.

Discovering that he was severely anemic, the pediatrician referred Brady to the local hospital. "We never in the world thought it would be cancer," Heather says, but a CT scan revealed a solid tumor in Brady's abdomen. Remembering the terrible

Continued on Page 2

Brady Burford

HILANDS' SIMPLE GIFT
Will Change Lives

Don and Joyce Hiland have something in common with thousands of people from across the United States and around the world—that's thousands of people whom they've never met. Don and Joyce support St. Jude Children's Research Hospital.

"We began getting items in the mail," Don says, "that led us to become interested in the hospital" and its conviction that no child should die in the dawn of life because of cancer or other catastrophic diseases.

St. Jude believes that all children deserve a chance at a life that's filled with love, laughter, friends and family—and they deserve such a chance regardless of the ability to pay.

The Hilands, who are both retired, came to share this belief and have used stock to establish a charitable gift annuity with St. Jude.

"St. Jude is a very good place and we are glad to help out," says Joyce, who notes that the payments she and Don receive are a very welcome supplement to their retirement income.

Establishing a gift annuity with St. Jude is easy and straightforward. Transfer cash or securities to the hospital and in return either you or as many as two annuitants that you name will receive lifetime payments. The principal eventually passes to St. Jude. As for the other benefits:
• You receive an immediate income tax deduction for a portion of your gift.
• Your lifetime annuity is backed by a reserve and the full assets of St. Jude Children's Research Hospital.

Continued on Page 3

Don and Joyce Hiland

p. 1

Illustration No. 7: Educational device from St. Jude Children's Research Hospital

donors and prospects. Its in-depth format shows the recipient that you take your gift-planning program seriously and that you're an enduring organization with the means to properly educate and cultivate your giving community – things you just can't accomplish with a "vehicle-oriented" postcard or an occasional letter from the chair of your board.

But whether you send a newsletter or other communication, your materials should look like someone cares enough to produce tasteful, but not lavish pieces.

• *The Offer*

Typically, organizations will offer to send a detailed brochure if the reader is interested in more information on a particular subject. Changing a few key words can give your offer added value. Rather than a brochure, offer "A Beginner's Guide" or a "An Estate Planning Toolkit." Also consider unique offers that will appeal to your specific audience: private campus tours, a free seat at an estate planning

Illustration No. 8: The offer of a free brochure

seminar, or a complimentary copy of your anniversary cookbook.

Too many gift planners fail to recognize the importance of including an intriguing offer. People who respond to an offer *of any kind* from your organization, whether they're asking for specific estate planning information or simply following up on a request to update their mailing address, distinguish themselves as "responders" who are open to furthering a relationship with you.

• ***The Reply Device***

A reply device provides donors with a means of responding to an offer (for an informational brochure, a premium gift, a campus tour) or of informing you of their intention to leave a gift in their estate plans. The traditional format is a freestanding card, which donors can return in a postage-paid, business reply envelope (BRE). Reply devices

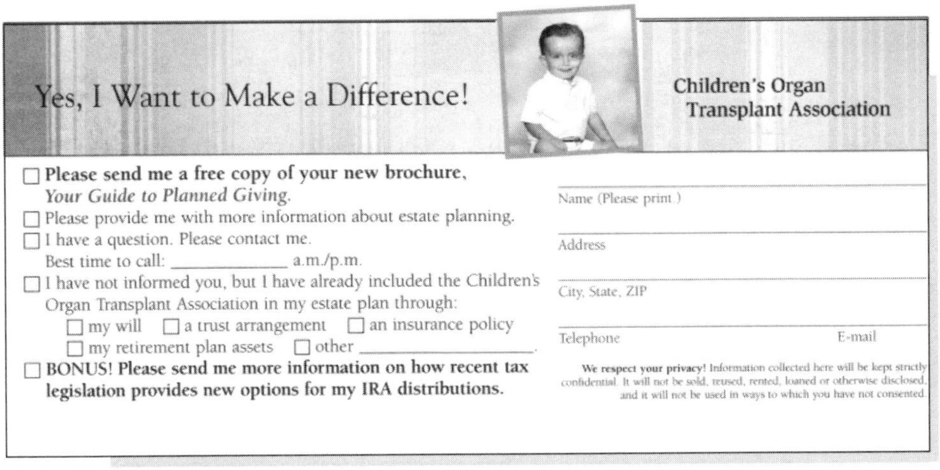

Yes, I Want to Make a Difference!

Children's Organ Transplant Association

☐ **Please send me a free copy of your new brochure, *Your Guide to Planned Giving*.**
☐ Please provide me with more information about estate planning.
☐ I have a question. Please contact me.
Best time to call: ____________ a.m./p.m.
☐ I have not informed you, but I have already included the Children's Organ Transplant Association in my estate plan through:
☐ my will ☐ a trust arrangement ☐ an insurance policy
☐ my retirement plan assets ☐ other ______________.
☐ **BONUS! Please send me more information on how recent tax legislation provides new options for my IRA distributions.**

Name (Please print.)

Address

City, State, ZIP

Telephone E-mail

We respect your privacy! Information collected here will be kept strictly confidential. It will not be sold, reused, rented, loaned or otherwise disclosed, and it will not be used in ways to which you have not consented.

Illustration No. 9: The reply device of Children's Organ Transplant Association

pre-printed with the donor's name and address will cost more to create, but will typically boost response.

Make it clear on the reply device that you hold personal information in confidence. Your materials need to encourage rather than discourage contact. Participants in our focus groups have expressed real concern that their personal information might be misused. You have everything to gain by making a clear statement that you don't sell or share donor information.

Our research has also shown that organizations must make it easy for donors to secure more information, on their own terms. We've encountered resistance from focus group participants about sending in a card to receive more information. In particular, younger donors (people in their 40s) are much more willing to visit websites to explore opportunities. Much of this preference stems from the desire to avoid disclosing personal information that might lead to unwanted contact. I'm not of the opinion, however, that the reply card should be wholly replaced with website information. Rather, I suggest organizations will benefit from opening numerous channels for communication, including websites, mail, and telephone.

■ Final Thoughts

In the 30-plus years I've been creating direct mail packages for gift planners, the proven formula outlined here has remained largely unchanged. Should we be alarmed by the seeming lack of innovation? Bored by the predictability of it all? Well, maybe. But we can't afford to overlook what still works.

The goal here is to develop a control package that can be counted on to perform every time – most likely based on some variation of the formula here. But the secret to successful direct mail is to constantly question what works, seek better results, develop innovative approaches and then test, test, test.

8

The Look

Every man I know owns a lucky tie. Mine is a crisp, vivid orange, and while it reflects my personality, it somehow enhances it, too. Every time I wear my orange tie, people seem to find me more handsome, with a quicker wit, even smarter. I feel like Super Me!

The look of your planned giving mailings should achieve the same result. First and foremost, your pieces should reflect the character of your organization.

Donors should instantly recognize – through a familiar logo, colors and layout – that this correspondence is from you. A look, feel, and tone that consistently reflect your organization's brand will comfort the reader and set the stage for ... Super You!

Super You is a newsletter or personal letter or brochure that reaches out and captures the hearts and minds of your donors. It's a connection they literally *feel* as they hold it in their hands, find themselves drawn to a particular photo or story, and decide then and there to act on something they've just read.

Creating materials that resonate with your audience requires careful attention to the elements of design. Color, paper, type style, type size, photos, graphics – these all play a critical role.

• Color

First, brighter is better. As vision declines with age, so does our ability to discriminate between colors, so it's no surprise that studies show people age 65 to 90 prefer bright colors to pastels (this also explains my Aunt Stella's choice in lipstick). Second, use color to complement your text, not compete with it. That means, above all, using black for the body of your text. Save color for your headlines, subheads, and pull quotes to attract attention and move the eye around the page.

• Paper

Print your materials on white paper. The high contrast of the white paper and black text provides much greater readability than printing on colored stock (see H vs. I on pp. 60 and 61). Choose a matte paper stock; glossy paper causes reflections that make reading more difficult.

• Type

An Australian magazine editor by the name of Colin Wheildon spent 10 years studying the way readers understand messages presented to them in a range of type styles and layouts. His findings are worth heeding.

Wheildon found that "pretty" fonts (think scrolls and calligraphy) are much too difficult to read. The same goes for sans-serif typefaces (those without little "feet" added to the main strokes of the letter form). Sans-serif fonts such as Helvetica and Arial, when used as the main text, are five times harder to read than serif body copy such as Garamond and Times New Roman (see pp. 60 and 61 - A vs. B). Save the san-serif type for headlines, subheads, pull quotes, and sidebars – it adds welcome contrast (C).

As for point size, keep your main text at a size comfortable for your readers. Ten- to 12-point type is a good starting point, but remember that 12-point type in one font can render an entirely different size than 12-point type in another. Let your naked eye be the judge.

Wheildon also cautions you to avoid reversing large blocks of text – white letters against a black background, for example (D vs. E). Further, take into consideration the leading, or space between the lines. Leading should be at least two to four points larger than the type size (e.g., 10-point type with 14-point leading, or 12-point type with 16-point leading). See A vs. B.

• Photos

The visual makes the first impact. Think of a photo as the enticement that brings the reader to the page. Let pictures tell the story, elicit emotion in your donors, and draw them to the articles for more information.

Try to avoid the worn-out, overused stock photos of picture-perfect seniors canoeing, gardening or bridge-playing their way into retirement (F). Photos from your own organization or pictures of your actual donors will be the most compelling (G). Close-up photographs are better attention grabbers. Cropping is also important. Poor cropping can ruin what could have been a great photo. Always include a caption, and let the caption tell the story. Often all that's read are the headlines and captions, so make them work!

BAD
LAYOUT

Summer 2007

Childrens
NONPROFIT PROGRAM

Visions

A Gift Planning Newsletter for Alumni and Friends of Our Organization

Giving to Our Organization

Have you considered establishing an endowment fund? As longtime organization supporters John and Jane Doe discovered, it's a powerful way to perpetually support a gift to us in your name or in the name of a loved one while realizing tax benefits for your kindness.

The Does made their gift to establish the Frank Doe Memorial Fund as a lasting tribute to John's father. They now have the satisfaction of knowing that Frank will be remembered while our organization will forever benefit from their gift.

More Information

An endowment program is simply the time-honored method of allocating certain gifts to an investment fund. This fund is invested to earn income each year, and as the principal grows, so does the income. That ever-growing income is used to support our work, but the principal always remains invested in order to perpetuate the fund.

When you make a gift to our endowment fund, it can either be outright or deferred (such as through a bequest in a will or living trust). Either way, your one gift can turn into a legacy of annual gifts long into the future.

Suppose you'd like to make sure your favorite charitable organization receives $1,000 every year, even after your lifetime. Let's say the charitable organization spends 5 percent of its endowment each year. (This doesn't mean it earns a cash return of only 5 percent, only that it spends that amount; it will reinvest the difference to offset inflation.)

To calculate the amount you need to donate to perpetuate your gift, divide the annual gift amount, $1,000, by the amount called for in the spending policy, 5 percent, and you get $20,000. So, contributing just $20,000 can continue the $1,000 annual gift indefinitely.

Here's the best part: If the value of the endowment fund grows beyond the spending amount, so does the income. For example, with a total return of 10 percent in one year and with only 5 percent spent, the other 5 percent is reinvested. By the second year, the value of the fund is 5 percent higher, or $21,000, and the "gift" from the fund is $1,050.

Conclusion
Endowment funds are a conservative and

intelligent attempt to guarantee the future of our mission and to enhance the quality of our opportunities for service. And they allow you to leave a legacy.

Contact our representative for more information about how your endowment gift can make a difference or our organization. Your inquiry is strictly confidential and without obligation, of course.

WILLS

If you are between 43 and 67 years of age, the National Association of Baby Boomers calls you one of its own. By some estimates, $41 to $136 trillion will be passed down to you from the estates your parents distribute.

Now, against a backdrop of terrorism and uncertainty over the future of Social Security, you may be more conscious than ever before—when creating or updating your well—about protecting much more than your money. Your will has to be about your survivors.

WILLS

If you are between 43 and 67 years of age, the National Association of Baby Boomers calls you one of its own. By some estimates, $41 to $136 trillion will be passed down to you from the estates your parents distribute.

Now, against a backdrop of terrorism and uncertainty over the future of Social Security, you may be more conscious than ever before—when creating or updating your well—about protecting much more than your money. Your will has to be about your survivors.

What You Own
Your will must be written, signed by you, and witnessed according to the laws of your state.

Select an attorney skilled in preparing wills in your state. Listen to suggestions about what you need to do to make your wishes start after your will visits.

Assess any assets that will pass through probate. Only property or assets in your name alone will pass to others under your will, making it important to know which assets pass under your will and which assets are distributed by other means. If you own property in "tenants in common" with someone, your share may be part of your probate estate. If you own property with someone jointly with rights of survivorship, however, that property will pass directly to that joint tenant—by type—right of your will, and not be included in probate.

Most life insurance proceeds and retirement plans aren't become part of your probate estate, but instead pass directly to your account's named beneficiary outside your will. These assets will also need to be coordinated as you prepare your overall estate plan.

Bequests
Who will receive your assets and your personal possessions? And why? Will your bequest help a broker than you intend to benefit? For example, certain types of inheritance carry adverse tax consequences.

Traditional and blended families alike have unique needs. Careful planning

ensures that everyone is remembered, and appropriately taken care of, with your will.

For many ideas with this will is a bequest to favorite charitable organization. There are many ways to stipulate this in your will. You can name a favorite charity in your will as a beneficiary of a specific dollar amount, or a specific asset or a portion of your estate.

Remember
Once you make your estate plan, you will soon realize that it is a good starting point. As your life changes, you will need to review your plans.

You may move to another state. Your relationships with individual family members may change. Your executor may die. You or a family member may become incapacitated. You may need to recognize the special needs of individuals. Review your will annually, or at least when family changes occur, and change if necessary.

Your plans for charitable giving may also change from time to time. A pre-wish, too, may find ways to benefit yourself and a charitable organization.

Make a Bequest

Benefiting your favorite educational, medical, arts, environmental, religious or other charitable organization will provide you with an enormous amount of satisfaction. How wonderful it is to know that after your death, your philanthropic ideals will continue to live by making a gift through your will.

Many people consider a bequest the perfect way to make a gift. You can help a charitable organization in the future without paying any of your assets today.

Advantages
A bequest lets you balance philanthropic goals with concerns that you may have about living expenses, future medical costs, and loved ones. Because you're not now really making a gift today and giving the fund today essentials, you need not worry that you won't have enough to live on sometime in the future should you need the next after all.

A bequest allows you the flexibility to use the asset if you need it. But at the same time, you become a partner in giving a concrete of an organization by promising a gift in the future.

What You Need
To make a bequest, you spend a certain and a revocable living trust. You can specify that the bequest be used for a certain purpose or you can make it an unrestricted gift. An unrestricted gift will be used where it is needed most.

Your gift can be made as either a specific bequest or as a percentage of your estate. Through a specific bequest, you give a certain amount of cash, securities, or property to the charitable organization. But, because most people do not know what the value of their estate will be at their death, making a gift to a charitable organization by using a percentage amount can be a more appropriate way to divide the estate. It allows you to benefit charitable organizations and individuals in relative proportion.

What to Do
- Determine if you need to update your will or revocable living trust.
- Select the charitable organization(s) you wish to benefit.
- Decide which purpose you want to support, or whether your gift will be made as an unrestricted gift.
- Notify the charitable organization of your intention to help, so we can thank you for your generous anonymous, as its staff can thank you for your gift and keep you informed of its ongoing activities.

"Satin's father would be proud to know that we chose such a wonderful way to honor him. An endowment was the perfect choice for us."
—Jane Doe

Many people consider a bequest the perfect way to make a gift. You can help a charitable organization in the future without using any of your assets today.

A bequest allows you the flexibility to use the asset if you need it. But at the same time you become a part of the giving community of an organization by promising a gift in the future.

It allows you to benefit charitable organizations and individuals in relative proportion.

The information in this publication is not intended as legal advice. For legal advice, please consult an attorney. Figures used in examples are based on current rates at the time of printing and are subject to change.

GOOD
LAYOUT

Summer 2007

Childrens NONPROFIT PROGRAM

Visions
A Gift Planning Newsletter for Childrens Nonprofit Program

A GIFT
That Lasts Forever

Have you considered establishing an endowment fund? As John and Jane Doe discovered, it's a powerful way to perpetually support a gift to us in your name or in the name of a loved one.

The Does made their gift to create the Frank Doe Memorial Fund as a lasting tribute to John's father. They now have the satisfaction of knowing that Frank will be remembered. Meanwhile, our organization will forever benefit from their gift.

How It Works

An endowment program is simply the time-honored method of allocating certain gifts to an investment fund. This fund is invested to earn income each year, and as the principal grows, so does the income. That growing income is used to support our work, but the principal always remains invested in order to perpetuate the fund.

When you make a gift to our endowment fund, it can either be outright or deferred (such as through a bequest in a will or living trust). Either way, your one gift can turn into a legacy of annual gifts long into the future.

Suppose you'd like to make sure your favorite charitable organization receives $1,000 every year, even after your lifetime. Let's say the charitable organization spends 5 percent of its endowment each year.

To calculate the amount you need to donate to perpetuate your gift, divide the annual gift amount, $1,000, by the amount called for in the spending policy, 5 percent, and you get $20,000. So, contributing just $20,000 can continue the $1,000 annual gift indefinitely!

Here's the best part: If the value of the endowment fund grows beyond the spending amount, so does the income. For example, with a total return of 10 percent in one year and with only 5 percent spent, the other 5 percent is reinvested. By the second year, the value of the fund is 5 percent higher, or $21,000, and the "gift" from the fund is $1,050.

Ask Us for Details

Endowment funds are a conservative and intelligent way to guarantee our future and enhance the quality of our opportunities for service. They also let you to leave a legacy.

John and Jane Doe established the Frank Doe Memorial Fund through an endowment gift to our organization.

YOUR WILL: A PLAN FOR SURVIVORS

If you are between 43 and 61 years of age, the National Association of Baby Boomers calls you one of its own. By some estimates, $41 to $136 trillion will be passed down to you from the estates your parents distribute.

Now, against a backdrop of international terrorism and uncertainty over the future of Social Security, you may be more conscious than ever—when creating or updating your will—about protecting much more than your money. Your will has to be about your survivors.

Assess What You Own And How You Own It

Your will must be written, signed by you and witnessed according to the laws of your state.

Select an attorney skilled in preparing wills in your state. Listen to suggestions about what you need to do to accomplish your goals.

Assess any assets that will pass through probate. Only property or assets in your name alone will pass to others under your will, making it important to know which assets pass under your will and which assets are distributed by other means. If you own property as "tenants in common" with someone, your share may be part of your probate estate. If you own property with someone jointly with rights of survivorship, however, that property will pass directly to that joint tenant—by law—outside of your will, and not be included in probate.

Most life insurance proceeds and retirement plans won't become part of your probate estate, but instead pass directly to your account's named beneficiary outside your will.

Bequests of All Kinds

Who will receive your assets and personal possessions? Will your bequests help or hinder those you intend to benefit?

You may also wish to make bequests to favorite charitable organizations. There are many ways to do that; some can benefit your family as well. We will be pleased to discuss with you how you can leave a bequest while also ensuring that your family will have the financial security they need.

Reasons to Review

Making your estate plan is a good starting point, but you will need to review your plans from time to time.

You may move to another state. Your relationships with individual family members may change. Your executor may die. You or a family member may become incapacitated. Review your will annually, or at least when family changes occur. Your plans for charitable giving may alter.

Remember

When you have made or revised your will, it may only be temporary. Time and events compel change. Make clear both by statement and by date when it was written. Also, be certain that someone knows where you keep your will.

Your will, once probated, becomes a matter of public record. Follow the basics. Let no error frustrate your ultimate intention to be considerate, generous and fair.

GOOD THINGS HAPPEN WHEN...
You Make a Bequest

Benefiting your favorite educational, medical, arts, environmental, religious or other charitable organization will provide you with an enormous amount of satisfaction.

Many people consider a bequest the perfect way to make a gift. You can help a charity in the future without using your assets today.

Great Flexibility

A bequest lets you balance philanthropic goals with concerns that you may have about living expenses, future medical costs and loved ones. Because you're not actually making a gift today and giving the asset away irrevocably, you need not worry that you won't have enough to live on should you need the asset after all.

How It Works

To make a bequest, you need a current will or revocable living trust. You can specify that the bequest be used for a certain purpose or you can make it an unrestricted gift.

Your gift can be made as either a specific bequest or as a percentage of your estate. Through a specific bequest, you give a certain amount of cash, securities or property. But, because most people do not know what the size of their estate will be at death, making a gift by using a percentage amount can be a more appropriate approach. It allows you to benefit individuals and charities in relative proportion.

To Make a Charitable Bequest

• Determine if you need to update your will or revocable living trust.
• Select the organization(s) you wish to benefit.
• Decide which purpose you wish to support, or whether your gift will be unrestricted.
• Notify the charity of your intention so its staff can thank you and keep you informed of its ongoing activities.

FOR MORE INFORMATION

John Doe
Director of Development
(123) 456-7890
john@childnp.org

www.childnp.org

12345 First Ave.
Des Moines, IA 50323
(800) 123-5432

Childrens NONPROFIT PROGRAM

CASE IN POINT
University of Georgia Foundation, Athens, Ga.

Keith Oelke, gift and estate planning executive director, has seen firsthand the difference photographs can make. The cover of the first newsletter he produced featured the publication's title and a stunning, full-page, four-color photo of the campus. A large photo of the featured donors dominated the inside spread; a foundation staff photo appeared on the back page. Keith still raves about the response to this mailing – results he attributes to the power of strong visuals. A picture truly can be worth a thousand words!

• Layout

Whether your means of communication is a newsletter, personal letter, postcard, or even a customized proposal, some layout principles are universally applicable:

• White space helps to move the reader's eyes around the page. Resist the temptation to cram.

• Make sure that all of the pieces your organization produces have some consistency in look and feel.

• Use a mix of fonts and font sizes to differentiate between headlines, subheads, and body copy. But don't overdo it. Typical layouts incorporate three font families.

• Choose photos and graphics that relate to the text rather than simply look pretty on the page. Always use captions to pull readers in.

• An oversized capital letter or small photo at the beginning of an article helps draw the eye to your intended starting point.

• Break up long blocks of text with subheads and pullout copy. Combining images with pullout copy further helps draw the reader's attention to key messages.

9

The Message

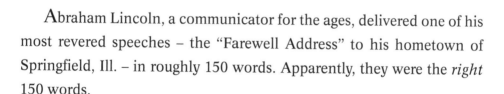

Abraham Lincoln, a communicator for the ages, delivered one of his most revered speeches – the "Farewell Address" to his hometown of Springfield, Ill. – in roughly 150 words. Apparently, they were the *right* 150 words.

Depending on the format you use, you'll have either more words (a typical newsletter has 1,200, for example) or fewer words than Lincoln (a postcard may allow only 50). No matter. You still want to choose yours as carefully as our esteemed 16th president.

■ A Winning Formula

A planned giving direct mail campaign typically serves one central purpose: To educate and inspire your donors. To that end, your message should include four types of content:

1) *A heartwarming story.* Usually a testimonial from someone who has supported your organization with a planned gift or has benefited from a donor's generosity.

2) *A case for giving.* Compelling information about your organization and its unique mission. What is the reason for your existence? How do you spend donors' money?

3) *Knowledge on which to act.* Instruction on general estate planning and perhaps an overview of a particular gift vehicle or two.

4) *A specific call to action.* A reason for your reader to take the next step, whether it's a special incentive to attend a seminar, a brochure that spells out certain information, or a reason to visit your website. Whatever your strategy, don't leave your readers without motivation to do something more.

Let's examine more closely each of these types of content.

■ Building the Story

Nothing in your mailing will burn brighter and longer in readers' minds than a real story of generosity. The gift described needn't be extravagant nor the recipient's situation especially dramatic. But a factor in nearly every donor's decision when considering a planned gift is the assurance that his or her dollars will be put to good use. Show them that you'll be worthy stewards of their generosity.

A testimonial from a donor can inspire your prospects to consider their own plans and help them understand basic planned giving concepts. Most people don't realize that creating such a gift doesn't require dipping into current cash flow or diverting inheritance away from family members. We've heard potential donors say, "Maybe I'll be able to do something like this once my mortgage is paid off," not realizing that planned gifts are fundamentally different from outright gifts of cash.

People need to see firsthand how others have accomplished their giving goals – whether it's the types of assets donors have used, what prompted them financially, what gift vehicles worked for their particular situations, or the impact they were able to have on organizations because of their generosity.

Make sure testimonials speak to the heart, as stirred emotions lead to gifts. Be careful, however. Our research shows that readers can be turned off by testimonials whose sole purpose is stroking the donor's ego ("Mr. Wilson's success in business provides him the freedom to travel the world...").

Consider one of my favorites:

> If you've ever doubted your ability to make a valuable difference in the world, consider the true story of Rose Guepfer, who was born on Oct. 22, 1902, deaf and mute, to a farm family from rural Wisconsin. Rose worked in the sewing room of Sacred Heart Hospital in Eau Claire, Wis., for 31 years. She mended surgical gowns and linens, never earning more than $6,100 a year before her retirement in 1988.
>
> With faltering prose, Rose once scribbled this note to an administrator: "I want to give money to hospital for sick people to come here to get well." When she died in 1997, Rose left the hospital her entire estate, worth more than $160,000. The money funded an endowment for the hospital's grief support center.

■ Making the Case

Your donors often spend years developing relationships with organizations before settling upon the one or two they'll ultimately support through a planned gift. The chosen few are those whose missions the donor finds most compelling or personally fulfilling, whose finances are the soundest, and whose stewardship of funds is impeccable.

Consider this statement from one of our focus group participants in Washington, D.C., in response to what he needs to hear from organizations in order to make a donation. This individual's views reflect a sentiment we've picked up on when talking with donors all over the U.S: "I don't appreciate generalities. I want them to say, 'This is what we've done this year ... we have this project and that project, and the other project.' I want them to lay out for me where my money will go."

Although you'll be sending your mailing to people who currently support your work to some degree, it remains critical to keep the *need for your existence* prominent in the minds of your donors. Reaffirm for them the impressive cause they've been supporting and thank them for their support. *But make sure you remind them of the needs yet to be fulfilled.*

■ Educating Your Audience

The meat of your communications will be the information you provide on estate planning and gift planning techniques (see Illustration 10). Planned gifts can seem complicated to the uninitiated, so this isn't the time to impress readers with your technical know-how.

Concentrate heavily on bequests and basic estate planning topics – these should form the foundation of each of your mailings. Include charts and example gift scenarios (see Illustration 11) to help illustrate your words.

Even if you're addressing a highly educated audience, you'll get better mileage out of articles that describe gift vehicles in clear, broad strokes than from overly technical pieces that intimidate people. Your correspondence doesn't have to include all the details now; your development officer or consultant can fill in the gaps later.

■ Calling Donors to Act

I'm a salesman at heart, so I'm always baffled when an organization doesn't include a call to action in its mailings for fear of insulting potential donors. People won't take the next step if

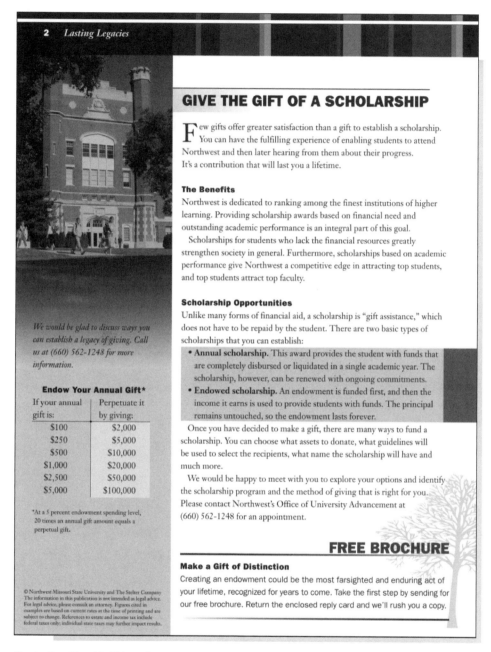

Illustration No. 10: Educational device from Northwest Missouri State University

you don't provide them a clear path.

Find reasons for your donors to take action. Include offers for additional information on subjects covered in your mailing, or an

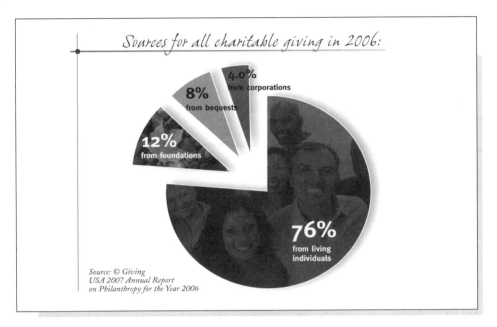

Sources for all charitable giving in 2006:

4.0% from corporations

8% from bequests

12% from foundations

76% from living individuals

Source: © Giving USA 2007 Annual Report on Philanthropy for the Year 2006

Illustration No. 11: The use of charts as a clarifying device for readers

invitation to tour your facility or attend a seminar, or a special incentive to visit your website. Give 'em a reason to act, and to act NOW.

■ A Final Word (or…79)

Once you've fine-tuned the 50-, 375- or 1,200-word lineup for your direct mail package – a carefully edited selection of emotionally rich and stimulating information – you will undoubtedly realize you forgot something. Or you'll look at the available white space on every page and feel compelled to fill it.

Stay the course, my friend! A finely tuned message – easily identified and digested – is far more effective than one buried among competing scraps of thought. Remember, space is precious, and less is often more. Amen.

10

Technically Speaking

———❖———

When it comes to technical expertise, gift planners usually fall into one of three camps:

1) Deer in the headlights who cringe at the thought of explaining the finer points.

2) Minor league players who are comfortable in their own shoes, but haven't reached the level of ...

3) Black belts who possess an exemplary level of skill and sometimes expect everyone else (their donors included) to share their passion for the obscurest details.

While it's important to recognize where you fit in with these camps, what's really key is to realize that the majority of your donors rank at the beginner level.

Depending on the maturity of your program, at least part of your audience is made up of people with only a vague understanding of the concept of gift planning. It's your job to raise awareness, pique interest, and inspire action. You can't do that by launching into arcane explanations in every communication you send.

Following is a two-phase sequence for introducing gift planning concepts and leading donors to higher levels of understanding.

■ Phase One

The central component of every gift planning program is bequests, and the precursor to making a bequest is creating a will. *Focus the attention of your beginner-level donors on this key action.*

Studies show that nearly 80 percent of all planned gifts come in the form of bequests. It stands to reason that the younger people are when they create a will, the likelier they'll be to include charitable bequests at some point in the future.

Furthermore, once people make bequests, they cross an important threshold, becoming prime candidates to increase their giving and to be more receptive to your solicitations. A number of large and successful programs focus almost exclusively on bequests in every mailing they send.

Next, among your donors and prospects promote the idea of their naming your organization as the beneficiary of life insurance policies, pensions, 401(k) plans, 403(b) plans, IRAs and similar plans.

Because of their heavy tax burden, retirement plan assets make ideal planned gifts and represent a huge opportunity for charitable organizations. In addition, because these gifts don't require a lawyer's assistance, they are among the easiest for donors to make. In fact, they can be accomplished through simple changes to beneficiary forms available from the account administrator or insurance company.

Also ranking high in popularity among planned gifts are charitable gift annuities. But caution is needed here. Most states

The Ease of Making a Bequest

You may have thought about including the North Carolina Symphony in your estate plan because we have been an important part of your life and your community. Although you can carry out this good intention in many ways, the easiest method is through a bequest in your will.

Here are three types of bequests:

1. **A specific bequest** leaves the recipient a specified amount of money or an identified item, such as a vacation home.
2. **A residuary bequest** disposes of all or a portion of assets remaining after everything specified in your estate has been distributed.
3. **A contingent bequest** designates that a beneficiary receives all or some of your estate dependent on a specific condition.

Most wills are not difficult or expensive to prepare. Unfortunately, many people put off doing so until it's too late. Wouldn't you rather take charge and have a will that says something about you and your values?

Your will allows you to provide security for family members and loved ones. Favorite possessions can be passed on to someone special. This vital document also provides a way to identify and support the causes and organizations that are important to you, like the North Carolina Symphony.

Sample Bequest Language

A specific bequest
"I leave the sum of $10,000 to the North Carolina Symphony."

A residuary bequest
"I leave 10 percent of all the rest, residue and remainder of my estate to the North Carolina Symphony."

A contingent bequest
"I give $10,000 to my nephew, John, if he is living, otherwise to the North Carolina Symphony."

"When we made our provision for the North Carolina Symphony, our daughter was still in elementary school. Because of anticipated financial demands as she grew, in particular college, and our desire to make a contribution to the Symphony, the best way to contribute and still stay on track with college and eventually retirement planning was to bequeath an amount in our wills to the Symphony."

–The Ferreira family,
Chapel Hill, NC

North Carolina Symphony Society, Inc.
4350 Lassiter at North Hills Avenue
Suite 250
Raleigh, NC 27609
(919) 733-2750
Fax: (919) 781-6066

Mary McFadden Lawson
Director of Special Campaigns
mlawson@ncsymphony.org
www.ncsymphony.org

Illustration No. 12: North Carolina Symphony's brochure encouraging bequest giving

regulate the offering of gift annuities. You must be registered in the state in which your organization operates and the state in which your donor lives. Check www.acga-web.org under "State

Illustration No. 13: Donors to the American Diabetes Association are encouraged to consider charitable remainder trusts.

Regulations" to be sure your organization is in compliance before you begin marketing gift annuities.

■ Phase Two

Although implementation of Phase One never ends – the gifts mentioned above should always be emphasized – you will reach a point at which donors may be ready to progress to more complicated gifts. This may not occur until your gift planning program has been in place for several years.

At that point, pull the trigger on Phase Two – the introduction of sophisticated gift types (see illustration 13). Trust-based gifts such as charitable remainder trusts and charitable lead trusts require a trustee, third-party administration, and the donor's consultation with an attorney. By their nature, these gifts can be more intimidating (for the donor and the development officer!).

Because our business revolves around financial transactions with far-reaching consequences, the burden of this responsibility naturally drives us to emphasize the technical details. But remember, the primary purpose of your message is to raise awareness, arouse interest and inspire action. Once you've accomplished that, you can always call in the SWAT team of technical experts to seal the deal.

11

A Matter of Time

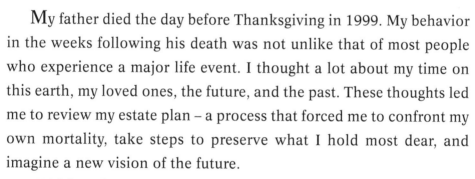

My father died the day before Thanksgiving in 1999. My behavior in the weeks following his death was not unlike that of most people who experience a major life event. I thought a lot about my time on this earth, my loved ones, the future, and the past. These thoughts led me to review my estate plan – a process that forced me to confront my own mortality, take steps to preserve what I hold most dear, and imagine a new vision of the future.

Within a few months, I established an endowed scholarship at the University of Iowa – the alma mater of my father, myself, and my two oldest sons. My father's passing had led me to open up in ways I wouldn't have imagined before.

■ Timing Is Everything

There are millions of donors like me who after a life changing event – whether a death, a birth, illness, retirement, or even the sale of a business – are ready to receive your message.

The problem is, life is unpredictable and you can't anticipate your donors' life-changing events. Therefore the best time to mail your materials is as often as you can afford. Timing is everything, and the more frequently you're in front of your loyal donors, the better.

Now for the reality check. You have a limited budget. You have opposing priorities. You have plenty of competing ideas on how to cultivate and inspire donors. In light of that, what is a realistic schedule?

Best-case scenario, you'll mail four times per year. Second-best scenario, you'll mail three times per year. Consider the following marketing calendar showing the coordination of mailings and other events.

SAMPLE MARKETING CALENDAR

January	Professional advisor luncheon
February	Planned giving mailing (newsletter or personal letter)
March	Professional advisor newsletter (Low-cost option: Mail a copy of a relevant article along with a personal note.)
April	Annual Legacy Society gathering
May	Planned giving mailing
June	Professional advisor newsletter (Low-cost option: Mail a copy of a relevant article along with a personal note.)
July	Gift planning article in organization's magazine; Professional advisor luncheon
August	Professional advisor newsletter or continual luncheon meetings with individual advisors
September	Planned giving mailing - Annual fund mailing
October	Professional advisor newsletter (Low-cost option: Mail a copy of a relevant article along with a personal note.)
November	Planned giving mailing
December	Invitation to fundraising event

Regardless of the schedule you develop for your own organization, do keep one important fact in mind. Americans contribute the majority of their charitable dollars (annual, major, or planned) in the last three months of the year. Make sure your fourth-quarter mailing lands in your donors' hands in October or November. You want to give them time enough to consider and implement a gift before the Dec. 31 tax deadline.

■ The Circle of Life

Not long ago my first grandchild was born to my oldest son. A few months later the second grandbaby arrived to my middle son. Though college is 18 years down the road, I'm already thinking about Benjamin and Samuel's education and the life they'll lead after I'm gone.

If ever a person was primed to update his estate plan and revise his vision of the future, once again it's me. The charitable organizations I include in this process are the ones that have stayed close through the years, reminding me of their mission, their needs, and their commitment to my dreams.

12

How to Improve Your Gift Planning Program in Five Easy Steps

——❖——

Way back in Chapter One, I promised to share with you a proven plan for your gift planning success. Well, here it is in all its elegant simplicity.

Step 1: Deal with the REAL Issues

It's human nature to elevate activities which bring us joy, or enhance us socially or professionally, or at which we excel. It's just as natural to avoid less interesting tasks. This explains how my wife can spend hours creating photo albums of family and friends, but never devote a single thought to changing the oil in her car.

If you want a gift planning program that runs on all cylinders, try to spend less time immersing yourself in this year's golf tournament, auction, or gala. Quit chasing the small gifts generated by a host of special events. Instead of organizing your desktop and cultivating office relationships, put your consistent energy into marketing your gift planning program.

■ Step 2: Keep in Touch during Times of Turnover

Staff turnover is a fact of life. And if you're not careful, it can quickly compromise your marketing program and dent relationships with donors. What message does it send to your most loyal supporters that your communication ceases when there's a personnel change?

It's not unusual for organizations to spend up to 12 months recruiting and training replacement staff, which puts the new hire a full year behind in the donor cultivation process. How many donors may have life-changing experiences during the time you're without a staffer?

Let go of the myth that your mailing program requires the skills of a senior officer. Until the new hire comes on board, retain a qualified consultant or professional advisor to follow up on your planned giving leads.

■ Step 3: Keep Your Direct Marketing Program on Task

Staff turnover isn't the only stumbling block adversely affecting the giving pipeline. Let me share another pitfall to avoid. If you're planning a capital campaign, common wisdom suggests delaying all other development efforts for the duration of the campaign.

But since only the top 10 percent to 20 percent of your donors are typically targeted for capital gifts, many of your best prospects for planned gifts will be ignored during the campaign. Your bucket of future estate gifts will begin to dry up. Avoid this by keeping your direct mail program active.

■ Step 4: Overcome Your Insecurities

Some fundraisers put off calling prospects because they're afraid they'll be asked a technical question they can't answer. I call this technical paralysis. But for goodness sake if this describes you, then enroll in a workshop or refresher course on the basics of gift planning. In the meantime, keep handy the phone numbers of gift planning attorneys and consultants who can advise you on the occasional tough question.

I've also come across my fair share of fundraisers who are downright afraid of talking with donors, due to their fear of rejection. Yes I know it requires some practice, but keep in mind that an initial rejection doesn't necessarily mean "no" (as opposed to "not yet").

One of my favorite rules of selling is that it takes eight calls to close a deal, but more than 80 percent of salespeople stop after the second call. I'm happy about those impatient salespeople – they leave a load of business for me.

Ironically, donor visits should be as comfortable as calling on old friends. This is your chance to thank them for their support, to share how their gifts have been used to make a difference, and to keep them in the loop about what's going on within your organization.

■ Step 5: Follow Up

When you receive a response from one of your marketing efforts, your follow-up effort should look like this:

1) Mail a personalized cover letter along with the requested information.

2) Follow up with a personal phone call or make an appointment for a visit.

3) Place the prospect on a list dedicated to "responders" – donors who by virtue of their responding to an offer elevate themselves to a higher level of interest.

4) Keep in personal contact with this donor (via phone call, mailing or letter) to a degree you deem appropriate – annually at a minimum.

■ See Your Gift Planning Program Improve

Overall success with the approach outlined here requires an unflagging belief in yourself and your mission. Stumbling blocks such as staff turnover, board impatience, and your own lack of follow-through can all chip away at your personal motivation and your program's results. But faithful adherence to these five steps will take your program to new heights ... eventually.

I recall in earlier days attending a professional conference. It was a big event with hundreds if not thousands of organizations present. Of those in the hall, just one - yes, one - was a client. I could have been embarrassed by our lack of penetration or intimidated by the formidable task ahead.

But after nearly 30 years of consistently executing the five easy steps outlined above, I'm proud to say that we've since won orders from more than 2,600 nonprofits. Heck, we could fill up our own hall now. That's not bragging, it's simply proof positive that keeping it simple does in fact pay off.

13

What Do You Expect? The Right Way to Measure Success

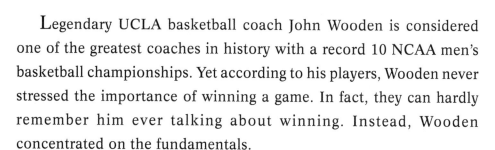

Legendary UCLA basketball coach John Wooden is considered one of the greatest coaches in history with a record 10 NCAA men's basketball championships. Yet according to his players, Wooden never stressed the importance of winning a game. In fact, they can hardly remember him ever talking about winning. Instead, Wooden concentrated on the fundamentals.

Those of us in the gift planning business could take a lesson from Wooden in the value of concentrating on fundamentals rather than the ultimate win. Besides, it's disheartening to gauge your short-term success on something that might take decades to come to fruition – especially when studies show that two-thirds of people who leave bequests *never* inform the organization of their intentions. You could already be a winner and not even know it!

That's easy for me to say, of course. I'm president of my own company. You on the other hand have a boss or a board to answer to and they want to know how to measure your success with planned giving.

Because every organization presents a unique set of circumstances – size of donor base, longevity of program, budget devoted to planned giving – it's impossible for me to suggest standard benchmarks. By networking with colleagues, participating in industry conferences and seminars, and joining online forums, you can begin to get a feel for what others in similar circumstances are achieving.

You might also consider an evaluation of your program – sometimes referred to as a planned giving audit or strategic assessment – conducted by an independent firm, which will point out your program's strengths and weaknesses and provide an action plan.

That said, here is a list of gift planning activities that organizations typically track:

• The number of new members added to your legacy society each year.

• The number of donors you contact each year via:
    -Letters
    -Emails
    -Phone calls
    -Personal visits

• The number of active prospects in your giving pipeline, along with where they are in the cultivation process.

• The number of planned gift proposals personally delivered to donors.

• The number of new planned gifts completed this year. List these as planned gift "expectancies." Note that the national average for a bequest gift is $48,000.

• The number of planned giving direct mail pieces you send and the response rates for each – whether by reply card, letter, phone call, or otherwise.

• Your ability to increase traffic on your website through promotions in your gift planning publications.

• The number of attendees at planned giving recognition events and educational events.

As for evaluating your relationships with professional advisors, you might track the following:

• How many educational lunches you host.

• How many direct mail pieces you send and the referral calls from each.

• The number of emails and telephone calls you make and receive.

• The number of referred prospects or donors you receive.

CASE IN POINT

Help! I can't see the forest for the trees!

A client in California called me one day upset about the low response to his gift planning newsletter. He was concerned that he'd received only five or six reply cards from his last issue. Knowing that success in this business isn't measured by response rates to a single mailing, I asked him how many new members he'd added to his legacy society in the past year. His answer: 15. Then I asked the amount of planned gifts he'd completed in the past year. His answer: $1.5 million.

We talked about the number of donor visits he was making and the volume of proposals he'd presented this year. As we looked at the fundamental metrics of his program, he realized he was indeed enjoying great success! The problem was that he was focusing on one factor – response rates – instead of the full breadth of activities that determine the ultimate success of a gift planning program.

■ Worth the Wait

Have patience with your program. It takes an average of seven years for a gift planning program to mature to the point where planned gifts are materializing, and it takes three to five qualified prospects to secure one planned gift.

In John Wooden's Pyramid of Success – which he used to guide dozens of teams to greatness and still serves as a model for athletes and business people today – "patience" and "faith" come together to form the apex of the pyramid.

Show patience, have faith, and follow the principles I've outlined in these pages, and in due time your success will follow.

14

Stay the Course

———❖———

Two of my sons, Nathan and Jeremy, both third-generation marketing consultants for our company, give me a hard time about how easy I make it look to sell our programs and services.

But as I always tell them, my success has less to do with my abilities and more to do with the fact that I've been building relationships for more than three decades. People trust me and know that when they're ready to start or revitalize their planned giving program, I'll be there to help.

This should be every organization's standard of commitment: to maintain continuity in marketing efforts to donors over the long haul – regardless of whether the organization is realizing immediate, short-term gain.

Too many boards embrace an 18-month mentality to funding their gift planning marketing. If their members can't see real, bottom-line results within that timeframe, they conclude it's too expensive to continue. But adopt this mentality and you'll rarely see planned gifts materialize.

CASE IN POINT
Show Me the Money

Karen Anderson, director of development at Hospice of Central Iowa in West Des Moines, Iowa, launched a gift planning program using a straightforward newsletter which she mailed every quarter for two years. Once she completed her eight-issue contract, I contacted her to renew the agreement and to broach the possibility of a more customized newsletter.

Karen informed me she couldn't continue because her board members demanded at a recent meeting that she "show them the money." The only evidence of success Karen could present was a small stack of reply cards from people saying they had put the hospice in their wills. The bad news, so to speak, was that all of these people were still alive. Based on the lack of concrete results, the board voted to terminate the program.

If I'd had the chance at the time, I would have kindly, but emphatically, explained to the board that most gift planning programs take three to five years of consistent marketing before a single dollar appears. I never got the chance ... but I did get vindication.

Four years later, I received an email from Karen asking me to visit with her again. "Why the renewed interest?" I asked upon arriving.

"The board asked me to call you," Karen replied. "Apparently the newsletter wasn't such a bad idea after all." She went on to explain that six of the 10 largest gifts the hospice received that year could be directly attributed to the direct mail program of four years earlier!

I asked Karen how she could be sure. "Since I've been here for eight years, I knew what we'd done in the past," she told me. "I recognized many of the donor's names and checked my files. Sure enough, three of them had told us we were included in their wills."

A board member then suggested that Karen check the dates when the other gifts had been drafted. Karen discovered that three people had completed their estate planning during that same two-year period. Although these individuals hadn't identified themselves through a reply card, it's likely they'd been motivated by her mailing to seek professional advice on making a gift.

I've seen this story repeated over and over across the country. Organizations begin communicating with their best donors but abandon the plan when they don't receive immediate gratification. This sends a terrible message to your best supporters, who are out there waiting for you to tell them what they can do next to strengthen your organization's mission.

APPENDIX

A) Benchmark Survey   93
B) Qualifying Call Summary Sheet (1)   95
C) Qualifying Call Summary Sheet (2)   97
D) Activity Reports   99

Benchmark Survey

This survey is suggested for use with new planned giving programs.
Send to your target audience to develop a baseline understanding of your
donors' familiarity with planned giving and disposition for giving.

In an effort to better meet the needs of our loyal donors, [Organization Name] is formally launching a planned giving program. Our goal is to provide you, our donors, and your financial advisors with the information you need to secure your financial futures and leave lasting legacies with the charitable causes you love.

We appreciate your feedback on how we might best meet your needs and provide the most appropriate information to all of our supporters. Please take a few minutes to fill out the short survey below.

1. Are you familiar with the term "planned giving"?   __Yes   __No

2. Are you aware of planned giving opportunities with [Organization Name]?   % Yes   % No

3. Have you received information from [Organization Name] regarding charitable estate planning ideas?   __Yes   __No

    If yes, in what form was that information presented to you?

    __ Newsletter
    __ Internet communication
    __ Alumni magazine
    __ Other _____

4. Have other organizations communicated with you about planned giving?   __Yes   __No

5. Would you like to receive financial planning ideas that would benefit you, your family and [Organization Name]?   __Yes __No

    If yes, what form of communication would you prefer?

    __ Print (newsletters, magazines)
    __ Internet based (e-mail, e-newsletters)
    __ Other _____

6. Have you ever considered a planned gift to [Organization Name]?
   __Yes __No

7. I have already included [Organization Name] in my estate plan through:
   __ My will
   __ My retirement plan assets
   __ A trust arrangement
   __ An insurance policy
   __ Other _____

Thank you for your feedback!

Name _____

Address_____

E-mail _____

Phone _____

Qualifying Call Summary Sheet (1)

*Use this form to help qualify prospects who have responded
to your marketing effort.*

Name _____

Phone _____

Spouse _____

Children _____

Donor age _____

Donor account no. _____

Giving history: _____ # of gifts

$ _____ Total amount given

Date of first gift: ____/____/____/

Date of call(s): ____/____/____/   ____/____/____/   ____/____/____/

In Response to a Marketing Lead

Date of original marketing mailing: ____/____/____/

Type of mailing: ___ Print ___ E-marketing

Gift type (i.e. bequest, charitable gift annuity):

_____ Send more information

_____ Considering this type of gift

_____ Already completed gift of this type

Conversation starters

"First, thank you for your support!"

"What prompted you to give?"

"What's your interest in the organization?"

Explain the impact of their gift.

"Is there further information I can provide?"

"Can I answer any questions or send additional materials?"

(Continued on next page)

Explain that you're trying to meet with your most loyal donors to learn more about why they give, hear their suggestions, and answer any question.

Comments: _____

_____

_____

_____

Next step: _____

_____

_____

_____

Qualifying Call Summary Sheet (2)

Use this form to help qualify prospects who have recently made a gift.

Name _____

Phone _____

Spouse _____

Children _____

Donor age _____

Donor account no. _____

Date of call(s): ____/____/____/   ____/____/____/   ____/____/____/

Date of gift ____/____/____/

Amount of gift $____

Conversation starters

"First, thank you for your support."

"What prompted your gift?"

"What's your interest in the organization?"

Explain the impact of the gift.

"Is there further information I can provide?"

Explain that you're trying to meet with your most loyal donors to learn more about why they give, hear their suggestions, and answer any questions.

Comments: _____

_____

_____

_____

Next step: _____

_____

_____

_____

Activity Reports

On the following three pages
are spreadsheet examples of ways
to track your daily activities and
the success of your marketing efforts.

1. *Print / Web Activity Report*
2. *Daily Activity Report*
3. *Print Campaign Activity Report*

Print / Web Activity Report: *By tracking both direct responses to your print campaigns and activity on your website, you'll develop a more comprehensive picture of the success of your marketing efforts.*

Promotional Package	Date Sent	Promotional Package Quantity	Direct Replies	% Response	Visitors to Website	Total % Web Response from Promotional Package	Total Responses	Total Response %	Gifts Received
(Newsletter, Postcard or E-Newsletter)			(Reply Cards, Phone Calls and E-mail)		(Check Web activity 10 days after drop date)		(Direct Replies and Web Response)		

Daily Activity Report: *A report of this type can be used to track your daily interactions with donors, including phone calls, emails, personal visits, and the proposals and informational materials you subsequently deliver.*

Print Package (Newsletter or Postcard)	Date Sent	Print Quantity	Direct Replies (Reply Cards, Web response, and Phone Calls)	% Response	New Recognition Club Members	Gifts Received

Print Campaigns Activity Report: *This form can be used to connect the dots between your marketing mailings and the results generated. Over time you should find a correlation between your marketing efforts and an increase in donor activity.*

DONOR CONTACT		CALLS			E-Mail SENT/ RECEIVED	VISITS				INFORMATION REQUESTED			
DONOR	DATE	ATTEMPTS	LEFT MESSAGE	CONVERSATIONS		SCHEDULED	NOT YETS	NO	YES	NO	YES	TYPE	DATE SENT

ACKNOWLEDGMENTS

Writing this book would have been infinitely harder without the dedication of my staff, who provided invaluable input along the way. In particular, I'd like to recognize: Johni Hays, J.D., Suzanne Mineck, Zach Christensen, Kristin Lensing, Dan Manderscheid, Patrick Smith, Russ Swanson and Steve Tuil. Most of all though, I would like to call attention to the endless hours of hard work and creative influence that Bev Hutney brought to the making of this book.

I'm grateful for the support and passion of my family with whom I work side by side every day: my wife and business partner, Peggy Fisher; my sons, Nathan and Jeremy Stelter; and my brother, Steve Stelter.

Finally, I would like to thank all of the clients and professional friends who allowed me to share their stories in the pages of this book. Their journeys have provided the backbone for this material. Without their dedication to the charities they serve, this book could never have been written.

The Gold Standard
In Books for Nonprofit Boards

Each can be read in an hour • Quantity discounts up to 50 percent

Fund Raising Realities Every Board Member Must Face
David Lansdowne, 112 pp., $24.95.

If every board member of every nonprofit organization in America read this book, it's no exaggeration to say that millions upon millions of additional dollars would be raised.

How could it be otherwise when, after spending just *one* hour with this gem, board members everywhere would understand virtually everything they need to know about raising major gifts. Not more, not less. Just exactly what they need to do to be successful.

In his book, *Fund Raising Realities Every Board Member Must Face: A 1-Hour Crash Course on Raising Major Gifts for Nonprofit Organizations*, David Lansdowne has distilled the essence of major gifts fund raising, put it in the context of 47 "realities," and delivered it in unfailingly clear prose.

Nothing about this book will intimidate board members. It is brief, concise, easy to read, and free of all jargon. Further, it is a work that motivates, showing as it does just how doable raising big money is.

Asking
Jerold Panas, 112 pp., $24.95.

It ranks right up there with public speaking. Nearly all of us fear it. And yet it is critical to our success. Asking for money. It makes even the stout-hearted quiver.

But now comes a book, *Asking: A 59-Minute Guide to Everything Board Members, Staff and Volunteers Must Know to Secure the Gift*. And short of a medical elixir, it's the next best thing for emboldening you, your board members and volunteers to ask with skill, finesse … and powerful results.

Jerold Panas, who as a staff person, board member and volunteer has secured gifts ranging from $50 to $50 million, understands the art of asking perhaps better than anyone in America. He knows what makes donors tick, he's intimately familiar with the anxieties of board members, and he fully understands the frustrations and demands of staff.

He has harnessed all of this knowledge and experience and produced a landmark book. What *Asking* convincingly shows — and one reason staff will applaud the book and board members will devour it — is that it doesn't take stellar communication skills to be an effective asker.

Nearly everyone, regardless of their persuasive ability, can become an effective fundraiser if they follow a few step-by-step guidelines.

Emerson & Church, Publishers
www.emersonandchurch.com

The Gold Standard in Books for Nonprofit Boards

The Fundraising Habits of Supremely Successful Boards
Jerold Panas, 108 pp., $24.95

Over the course of a storied career, Jerold Panas has worked with literally thousands of boards, from those governing the toniest of prep schools to those spearheading the local Y. He has counseled floundering groups; he has been the wind beneath the wings of boards whose organizations have soared.

In fact, it's a safe bet that Panas has observed more boards at work than perhaps anyone in America, all the while helping them to surpass their campaign goals of $100,000 to $100 million.

Funnel every ounce of that experience and wisdom into a single book and what you end up with is *The Fundraising Habits of Supremely Successful Boards*, the brilliant culmination of what Panas has learned firsthand about boards who excel at the task of resource development.

Fundraising Habits offers a panoply of habits any board would be wise to cultivate. Some are specific, with measurable outcomes. Others are more intangible, with Panas seeking to impart an attitude of success.

In all, there are 25 habits and each is explored in two- and three-page chapters … all of them animated by real-life stories only this grandmaster of philanthropy can tell.

Fund Raising Mistakes that Bedevil All Boards (& Staff Too)
Kay Sprinkel Grace, 112 pp., $24.95

Fundraising mistakes are a thing of the past. Or, rather, there's no excuse for making one anymore. If you blunder from now on, it's simply evidence you haven't read Kay Grace's book, in which she exposes *all* of the costly errors that thwart us time and again.

Some, like the following, may be second nature to you:
• "Tax deductibility is a powerful incentive." It isn't, as you perhaps know.
• "People will give just because yours is a good cause." They won't.
• "Wealth is mostly what determines a person's willingness to give." Not really. Other factors are equally important.

Other mistakes aren't as readily apparent. For example: "You need a powerful board to have a successful campaign." Truth be told, many are convinced that without an influential board they can't succeed. Grace shows otherwise.

Then, too, there are more nuanced mistakes:
• "We can't raise big money - we don't know any rich people." Don't believe it. You can raise substantial dollars.
• "Without a stable of annual donors, you can't have a successful capital campaign." In fact you can, but your tactics will be different.
• "You need a feasibility study before launching a capital campaign." Turns out, you might not.

Emerson & Church, Publishers
www.emersonandchurch.com

The Gold Standard in Books for Nonprofit Boards

Big Gifts for Small Groups
Andy Robinson, 112 pp., $24.95

If yours is among the tens of thousands of organizations for whom six- and seven-figure gifts are unattainable, then Andy Robinson's book, *Big Gifts for Small Groups*, is just the ticket for you and your board.

Robinson is the straightest of shooters and there literally isn't one piece of advice in this book that's glib or inauthentic. As a result of Robinson's 'no bull' style, board members will instantly take to the book, confident the author isn't slinging easy bromides.

They'll learn everything they need to know from this one-hour read: how to get ready for the campaign, whom to approach, where to find them; where to conduct the meeting, what to bring with you, how to ask, how to make it easy for the donor to give, what to do once you have the commitment – even how to convey your thanks in a memorable way.

Believing that other books already focus on higher sum gifts, the author wisely targets a range that's been neglected: $500 to $5,000.

Robinson has a penchant for good writing and for using precisely the right example or anecdote to illustrate his point. But more importantly he lets his no-nonsense personality shine through. The result being that by the end of the book, board members just may turn to one another and say, "Hey, we can do this" – and actually mean it.

How Are We Doing?
Gayle Gifford, 120 pp., $24.95

Ah, simplicity.
That's not a word usually voiced in the same breath as 'board evaluation.'
Or brevity … and clarity … and cogency.
Yet all four aptly describe Gayle Gifford's book, *How Are We Doing: A 1-Hour Guide to Evaluating Your Performance as a Nonprofit Board*.

Until now, almost all books dealing with board evaluation have had an air of unreality about them. The perplexing graphs, the matrix boxes, the overlong questionnaires. It took only a thumbing through to render a judgment: "My board's going to use this? Get real!"

Enter Gayle Gifford. She has pioneered an elegantly simple and enjoyable way for boards to evaluate *and* improve their overall performance. It all comes down to answering some straightforward questions.

It doesn't matter whether the setting is formal or casual, whether you have 75 board members or seven, or whether yours is an established institution or a grassroots start-up. All that matters is that the questions are answered candidly and the responses openly discussed.

Emerson & Church, Publishers
www.emersonandchurch.com

The Gold Standard in Books for Nonprofit Boards

Great Boards for Small Groups
Andy Robinson, 112 pp., $24.95

Yours is a good board, but you want it to be better.
• You want clearly defined objectives …
• Meetings with more focus …
• Broader participation in fundraising …
• And more follow-through between meetings.

You want these and a dozen other tangibles and intangibles that will propel your board from good to great. Say hello to your guide, Andy Robinson, who has a real knack for offering "forehead-slapping" solutions – "Of course! Why haven't we been doing this?"

Take what he calls the "Fundraising Menu." Here, board members are asked to generate a list of all the ways (direct and indirect) they could assist in fundraising. The list is prioritized and then used to help each trustee prepare a personalized fundraising agreement meeting his specific needs.

Simple, right? Yet the Fundraising Menu is the closest thing you'll find to guaranteeing a board's commitment to raising money.

Great Boards for Small Groups contains 31 brief chapters. In fact the whole book can be read in an hour. Funny thing, its impact on those who heed its advice will last for years.

The Ultimate Board Member's Book
Kay Sprinkel Grace, 114 pp., $24.95

Here is a book for *all* of your board members:
• Those needing an orientation to the unique responsibilities of a nonprofit board,
• Those wishing to clarify exactly what their individual role is,
• Those hoping to fulfill their charge with maximum effectiveness.

Kay Sprinkel Grace's perceptive work will take board members just one hour to read, and yet they'll come away from *The Ultimate Board Member's Book* with a firm command of just what they need to do to help your organization succeed.

It's all here in 114 tightly organized and jargon-free pages: how boards work, what the job entails, the time commitment involved, the role of staff, serving on committees and task forces, fundraising responsibilities, conflicts of interest, group decision-making, effective recruiting, de-enlisting board members, board self-evaluation, and more.

In sum, everything a board member needs to know to serve knowledgeably is here.

Emerson & Church, Publishers
www.emersonandchurch.com

INDEX

AARP, 26

American Diabetes Association,
   72

American Society for the
Prevention of Cruelty to
   Animals, 36

Anderson, Karen, 88

Children's Hospital and Health
   System, 48

Children's Organ Transplant
   Association, 51, 54

Child*Serve*, 41

Cleveland Orchestra, *The*, 47

Dallas K. Beal Legacy Society,
   49

Design,
  -elements of, 58-62

Dierks, David, 19

Direct mail,
   -package and components,
   45-55

*Direct Marketing Association's
   Statistical Fact Book*, 47

Direct marketing formula, 25

Einstein, Albert, 23

Financial Planning Assoc., 41

Fruit, Sandi, 37

Goldberg, Bob, 21

Guepfer, Rose, 65

Hays, Johni, 40-41

Hospice of Central Iowa, 88

Indiana Univ. Center on
   Philanthropy, 35

Johnston, Julie, 14

Johnston, Steven, 23

Kansas State University, 37

King, Billie Jean, 35

Lincoln, Abraham, 63

Mailing,
   -budgeting, 28
   -characteristics of recipients,
     25-28, 29-33
   -goals of, 17-22

Mankato State University, 21

Marketing calendar, 76

Mega Gifts, 17

Mercy Hospital Foundation, 14

Metzler, Howard, 22

Mothers Against Drunk Driving,
   48

National Association of Estate
   Planners, 41

North Carolina Symphony, 71
Northwest Missouri State
　University, 67
Oelke, Keith, 62
Panas, Jerold, 17-18
People Magazine, 18
Philanthropy
　-women in, 35-38
Pomona College, 22
Professional advisors, 39-43
Pyramid of Success, 86
Riggs, Bobby, 35
Sacred Heart Hospital, 65
Schroeder-Scott, Grace, 18

Society of Financial Service
　Professionals, 42
Stelter, Jeremy, 87
Stelter, Nathan, 31, 87
St. Jude Children's Research
　Hospital, 52
St. Olaf College, 18
St. Mary's Duluth Clinic, 23
Thomas College, 50
University of Georgia
　Foundation, 62
University of Iowa, 19, 75
U.S. Census Bureau, 36
Wheildon, Colin, 58-59
Wooden, John 83, 86

Emerson
& Church
PUBLISHERS